Ansible Configuration Management

Leverage the power of Ansible to quickly configure your Linux infrastructure with ease

Daniel Hall

BIRMINGHAM - MUMBAI

Ansible Configuration Management

First published: November 2013

Production Reference: 1151113

Published by Packt Publishing Ltd.
Livery Place
35 Livery Street
Birmingham B3 2PB, UK.

ISBN 978-1-78328-081-0

www.packtpub.com

Cover Image by Prashant Timappa Shetty (sparkling.spectrum.123@gmail.com)

Credits

Author
Daniel Hall

Reviewers
Niels Dequeker
Lex Toumbourou

Acquisition Editor
Pramila Balan
Gregory Wild

Commissioning Editor
Deepika Singh

Technical Editors
Novina Kewalramani
Rohit Kumar Singh

Copy Editors
Roshni Banerjee
Mradula Hegde
Laxmi Subramaniam

Project Coordinator
Suraj Bist

Proofreader
Maria Gould

Indexer
Rekha Nair

Graphics
Ronak Dhruv

Production Coordinators
Aditi Gajjar
Arvindkumar Gupta
Adonia Jones

Cover Work
Aditi Gajjar
Adonia Jones

About the Author

Daniel Hall started as a Systems Administrator at RMIT University after completing his Bachelor of Computer Science degree there in 2009. More recently, he has been working to improve the deployment processes at `realestate.com.au`. Like many System Administrators, he is constantly trying to make his job easier and easier, and has been using Ansible to this effect.

I would like to thank my partner, Kate, for her continued support when I was writing this book. I would also like to thank my reviewers for their insightful corrections. Finally, I would like to thank everybody at Packt for giving me this opportunity and helping this first time author navigate the world of writing.

About the Reviewers

Niels Dequeker is a frontend developer who's passionate about the Web.

Currently, he's working with the JavaScript Research and Development team at Hippo, a company based in the beautiful city center of Amsterdam. He's responsible for the realization of the Hippo CMS, giving advice to both colleagues and clients about the possibilities and solutions.

Niels has used Ansible in a production environment, for both Server Configuration and Application Deployment.

He is also co-organizer of the JavaScript MVC Meetup in Amsterdam, where people come together monthly to share, inspire, and learn.

Lex Toumbourou has worked in the Information Technology field for over 8 years, in a career centered on System Engineering and Software Development. Though he turned his focus on Ansible recently, Lex has worked with Puppet, Nagios, RRD, Fabric, Django, Postgres, Splunk, Git, the Python ecosystem, the PHP ecosystem, and everything in between. Lex is an avid supporter of DevOps and loves automation and analytics.

I would like to thank my girlfriend, Kelly Seu, for putting up with me during one of the craziest years of my life. Love you so much.

www.PacktPub.com

Support files, eBooks, discount offers and more

You might want to visit www.PacktPub.com for support files and downloads related to your book.

Did you know that Packt offers eBook versions of every book published, with PDF and ePub files available? You can upgrade to the eBook version at www.PacktPub.com and as a print book customer, you are entitled to a discount on the eBook copy. Get in touch with us at service@packtpub.com for more details.

At www.PacktPub.com, you can also read a collection of free technical articles, sign up for a range of free newsletters and receive exclusive discounts and offers on Packt books and eBooks.

http://PacktLib.PacktPub.com

Do you need instant solutions to your IT questions? PacktLib is Packt's online digital book library. Here, you can access, read and search across Packt's entire library of books.

Why Subscribe?

- Fully searchable across every book published by Packt
- Copy and paste, print and bookmark content
- On demand and accessible via web browser

Free Access for Packt account holders

If you have an account with Packt at www.PacktPub.com, you can use this to access PacktLib today and view nine entirely free books. Simply use your login credentials for immediate access.

Table of Contents

Preface

Since CFEngine was first created by Mark Burgess in 1993, configuration management tools have been constantly evolving. Followed by the emergence of more modern tools such as Puppet and Chef, there are now a large number of choices available to a system administrator.

Ansible is one of the newer tools to arrive into the configuration management space. Where other tools have focused on completeness and configurability, Ansible has bucked the trend and, instead, focused on simplicity and ease of use.

In this book, we aim to show you how to use Ansible from the humble beginnings of its CLI tool, to writing playbooks, and then managing large and complex environments. Finally, we teach you how to extend Ansible by writing your own modules.

What this book covers

Chapter 1, Getting Started with Ansible, teaches you the basics of Ansible, how to build an inventory, how to use modules, and, most importantly, how to get help.

Chapter 2, Simple Playbooks, teaches you how to combine multiple modules to create Ansible playbooks to manage your hosts.

Chapter 3, Advanced Playbooks, delves deeper into Ansible's scripting language and teaches you more complex language constructs.

Chapter 4, Larger Projects, teaches you the techniques to scale Ansible configurations to large deployments containing many complicated systems.

Chapter 5, Custom Modules, teaches you how to expand Ansible beyond its current capabilities.

What you need for this book

To use this book, you will need at least the following:

- A text editor
- A machine with Linux operating system
- Python 2.6.x

However, to use Ansible to its full effect, you should have several Linux machines available to be managed. You could use a virtualization platform to simulate many hosts, if required.

Who this book is for

This book is intended for those who want to understand the basics of how Ansible works. It is expected that you have rudimentary knowledge of how to set up and configure Linux machines. In parts of the book, we cover the configuration files of BIND, MySQL, and other Linux daemons; a working knowledge of these would be helpful, but is certainly not required.

Conventions

In this book, you will find a number of styles of text that distinguish between different kinds of information. Here are some examples of these styles, and an explanation of their meaning.

Code words in text are shown as follows: "We can include other contexts through the use of the `include` directive."

A block of code is set as follows:

```
[group]
machine1
machine2
machine3
```

When we wish to draw your attention to a particular part of a code block, the relevant lines or items are set in bold:

```
tasks:
  - name: install apache
    action: yum name=httpd state=installed

  - name: configure apache
    copy: src=files/httpd.conf dest=/etc/httpd/conf/httpd.conf
```

Any command-line input or output is written as follows:

```
ansible machinename -u root -k -m ping
```

New terms and **important words** are shown in bold.

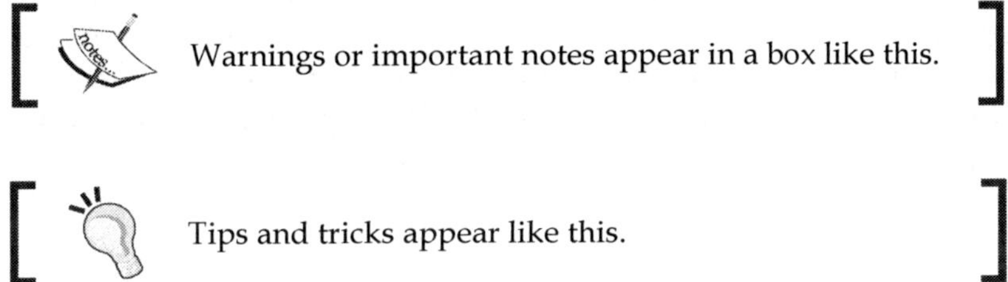

Reader feedback

Feedback from our readers is always welcome. Let us know what you think about this book—what you liked or may have disliked. Reader feedback is important for us to develop titles that you really get the most out of.

To send us general feedback, simply send an e-mail to `feedback@packtpub.com`, and mention the book title via the subject of your message.

If there is a topic that you have expertise in and you are interested in either writing or contributing to a book, see our author guide on `www.packtpub.com/authors`.

Customer support

Now that you are the proud owner of a Packt book, we have a number of things to help you to get the most from your purchase.

Downloading the example code

You can download the example code files for all Packt books you have purchased from your account at `http://www.packtpub.com`. If you purchased this book elsewhere, you can visit `http://www.packtpub.com/support` and register to have the files e-mailed directly to you.

Errata

Although we have taken every care to ensure the accuracy of our content, mistakes do happen. If you find a mistake in one of our books—maybe a mistake in the text or the code—we would be grateful if you would report this to us. By doing so, you can save other readers from frustration and help us improve subsequent versions of this book. If you find any errata, please report them by visiting `http://www.packtpub.com/submit-errata`, selecting your book, clicking on the **errata submission form** link, and entering the details of your errata. Once your errata are verified, your submission will be accepted and the errata will be uploaded on our website, or added to any list of existing errata, under the Errata section of that title. Any existing errata can be viewed by selecting your title from `http://www.packtpub.com/support`.

Piracy

Piracy of copyright material on the Internet is an ongoing problem across all media. At Packt, we take the protection of our copyright and licenses very seriously. If you come across any illegal copies of our works, in any form, on the Internet, please provide us with the location address or website name immediately so that we can pursue a remedy.

Please contact us at `copyright@packtpub.com` with a link to the suspected pirated material.

We appreciate your help in protecting our authors, and our ability to bring you valuable content.

Questions

You can contact us at `questions@packtpub.com` if you are having a problem with any aspect of the book, and we will do our best to address it.

1
Getting Started with Ansible

Ansible is profoundly different from other configuration management tools available today. It has been designed to make configuration easy in almost every way, from its simple English configuration syntax to its ease of set up. You'll find that Ansible allows you to stop writing custom configuration and deployment scripts and lets you simply get on with your job.

Ansible only needs to be installed on the machines that you use to manage your infrastructure. It does not need a client to be installed on the managed machine nor does it need any server infrastructure to be set up before you can use it. You should even be able to use it merely minutes after it is installed, as we will show you in this chapter.

You will be using Ansible from the command line on one machine, which we will call the **controller machine**, and use it to configure another machine, which we will call the **managed machine**. Ansible does not place many requirements on the controller machine and even less on the managed machine.

The requirements for the controller machine are as follows:

- Python 2.6 or higher
- paramiko
- PyYAML
- Jinja2

The managed machine needs **Python 2.4** or higher and **simplejson**; however, if your **Python** is **2.6** or higher, you only need **Python**.

The following are the topics covered in this chapter:

- Installing Ansible
- Configuring Ansible
- Using Ansible from the command line
- How to get help

Installation methods

If you want to use Ansible to manage a set of existing machines or infrastructure, you will likely want to use whatever package manager is included on those systems. This means that you will get updates for Ansible as your distribution updates it, which may lag several versions behind other methods. However, it doesn't mean that you will be running a version that has been tested to work on the system you are using.

If you run an existing infrastructure but need a newer version of Ansible, you can install Ansible via **pip**. Pip is a tool used to manage packages of Python software and libraries. Ansible releases are pushed to pip as soon as they are released, so if you are up to date with pip, you should always be running the latest version.

If you imagine yourself developing lots of modules and possibly contributing back to Ansible, you should be running a checked-out version. As you will be running the latest and least tested version of Ansible, you may experience a hiccup or two.

Installing from your distribution

Most modern distributions include a package manager that automatically manages package dependencies and updates for you. This makes installing Ansible via your package manager by far the easiest way to get started with Ansible; usually it takes only a single command. It will also be updated as you update your machine, though it may be a version or two behind. The following are the commands to install Ansible on the most common distributions. If you are using something different, refer to the user guide for your package or your distribution's package lists.

- **Fedora, RHEL, CentOS, and compatible**: `$ yum install ansible`
- **Ubuntu, Debian, and compatible**: `$ apt-get install ansible`

Installing from pip

Pip, like a distribution's package manager, will handle finding, installing, and updating the packages you ask for and its dependencies. This makes installing Ansible via pip as easy as installing from your package manager. It should be noted, however, that it will not be updated with your operating system. Additionally, updating your operating system may break your Ansible installation; however, this is unlikely. The following is the command to install Ansible via pip:

```
$ pip install ansible
```

Installing from the source code

Installing from the source code is a great way to get the latest version, but it may not be tested as correctly as released versions. You also will need to take care of updating to newer versions yourself and making sure that Ansible will continue to work with your operating system updates. To clone the `git` repository and install it, run the following commands. You may need root access to your system to do this:

```
$ git clone git://github.com/ansible/ansible.git
$ cd ansible
$ sudo make install
```

Setting up Ansible

Ansible needs to be able to get an inventory of the machines that you want to configure in order to manage them. This can be done in many ways due to inventory plugins. Several different inventory plugins are included with the base install. We will go over these later in the book, but for now we will cover the simple hosts file inventory.

The default Ansible inventory file is named hosts and placed in `/etc/ansible`. It is formatted like an INI file. Group names are enclosed in square braces, and everything underneath it, down to the next group heading, gets assigned to that group. Machines can be in many groups at one time. Groups are used to allow you to configure many machines at once. You can use a group instead of a hostname as a host pattern in later examples, and Ansible will run the module on the entire group at once.

In the following example, we have three machines in a group named `webservers`, namely `site01`, `site02`, and `site01-dr`. We also have a `production` group that consists of `site01`, `site02`, `db01`, and `bastion`.

```
[webservers]
site01
site02
```

```
site01-dr

[production]
site01
site02
db01
bastion
```

Once you have placed your hosts in the Ansible inventory, you can start running commands against them. Ansible includes a simple module called `ping` that lets you test connectivity between yourself and the host. Let's use Ansible from the command line against one of our machines to confirm that we can configure them.

Ansible was designed to be simple and one of the ways the developers have done this is by using SSH to connect to the managed machines. It then sends the code over the SSH connection and executes it. This means that you don't need to have Ansible installed on the managed machine. It also means that Ansible can use the same channels that you are already using to administer the machine.

First, we check connectivity to our server to be configured using the Ansible `ping` module. This module simply connects to the following server:

```
$ ansible site01 -u root -k -m ping
```

This should ask for the SSH password and then produce a result that looks like the following code:

```
site01 | success >> {
  "changed": false,
  "ping": "pong"
}
```

If you have an SSH key set up for the remote system, you will be able to leave off the `-k` argument to skip the prompt and use the keys. You can also configure Ansible to use a particular username all the time by either configuring it in the inventory on a per host basis or in the global Ansible configuration.

To set the username globally, edit `/etc/ansible/ansible.cfg` and change the line that sets `remote_user` in the `[defaults]` section. You can also change `remote_port` to change the default port that Ansible will SSH to. These will change the default settings for all the machines, but they can be overridden in the inventory file on a per server or per group basis.

To set the username in the inventory file, simply append ansible_ssh_user to the line in the inventory. For example, the next code section shows an inventory where the site01 host uses the username root and the site02 host uses the username daniel. There are also other variables you can use. The ansible_ssh_host file allows you to set a different hostname and the ansible_ssh_port file allows you to set a different port; this is demonstrated on the site01-dr host. Finally, the db01 host uses the username fred and also sets a private key using ansible_ssh_private_key_file.

```
[webservers]       #1
site01 ansible_ssh_user=root      #2
site02 ansible_ssh_user=daniel      #3
site01-dr ansible_ssh_host=site01.dr ansible_ssh_port=65422      #4
[production]       #5
site01       #6
site02       #7
db01 ansible_ssh_user=fred
ansible_ssh_private_key_file=/home/fred/.ssh.id_rsa bastion      #8
```

If you aren't comfortable with giving Ansible direct access to the root account on the managed machines, or your machine does not allow SSH access to the root account (such as Ubuntu's default configuration), you can configure Ansible to obtain root access using sudo. Using Ansible with sudo means that you can enforce auditing the same way you would otherwise. Configuring Ansible to use sudo is as simple as it is to configure the port, except that it requires sudo to be configured on the managed machine.

The first step is to add a line to the /etc/sudoers file; this may already be set up if you choose to use your own account. You can use a password with sudo, or you can use a passwordless sudo. If you decide to use a password, you will need to use the -k argument to Ansible, or set the ask_sudo_pass value to true in /etc/ansible/ansible.cfg. To make Ansible use sudo, add --sudo to the command line.

First steps with Ansible

Ansible modules take arguments in key value pairs that look similar to key=value, perform a job on the remote server, and return information about the job as JSON. The key value pairs allow the module to know what to do when requested. They can be hard coded values, or in playbooks they can use variables, which will be covered in *Chapter 2, Simple Playbooks*. The data returned from the module lets Ansible know if anything changed or if any variables should be changed or set afterwards.

Modules are usually run within playbooks as this lets you chain many together, but they can also be used on the command line. Previously, we used the `ping` command to check that Ansible had been correctly setup and was able to access the configured node. The `ping` module only checks that the core of Ansible is able to run on the remote machine but effectively does nothing.

A slightly more useful module is called setup. This module connects to the configured node, gathers data about the system, and then returns those values. This isn't particularly handy for us while running from the command line, however, in a playbook you can use the gathered values later in other modules.

To run Ansible from the command line, you need to pass two things, though usually three. First is a **host pattern** to match the machine that you want to apply the module to. Second you need to provide the name of the module that you wish to run and optionally any arguments that you wish to give to the module. For the host pattern, you can use a group name, a machine name, a glob, and a tilde (~), followed by a regular expression matching hostnames, or to symbolize all of these, you can either use the word `all` or simply `*`.

To run the `setup` module on one of your nodes, you need the following command line:

```
$ ansible machinename -u root -k -m setup
```

The `setup` module will then connect to the machine and give you a number of useful facts back. All the facts provided by the `setup` module itself are prepended with `ansible_` to differentiate them from variables. The following is a table of the most common values you will use, example values, and a short description of the fields:

Field	Example	Description
`ansible_architecture`	`x86_64`	The architecture of the managed machine
`ansible_distribution`	`CentOS`	The Linux or Unix distribution on the managed machine
`ansible_distribution_version`	`6.3`	The version of the preceding distribution
`ansible_domain`	`example.com`	The domain name part of the server's hostname
`ansible_fqdn`	`machinename.example.com`	This is the fully qualified domain name of the managed machine
`ansible_interfaces`	`["lo", "eth0"]`	A list of all the interfaces the machine has, including the loopback interface

Field	Example	Description
ansible_kernel	2.6.32-279.el6.x86_64	The kernel version installed on the managed machine
ansible_memtotal_mb	996	The total memory in megabytes available on the managed machine
ansible_processor_count	1	The total CPUs available on the managed machine
ansible_virtualization_role	guest	Whether the machine is a guest or a host machine
ansible_virtualization_type	kvm	The type of virtualization setup on the managed machine

These variables are gathered using Python from the host system; if you have **facter** or **ohai** installed on the remote node, the setup module will execute them and return their data as well. As with other facts, ohai facts are prepended with `ohai_` and facter facts with `facter_`. While the setup module doesn't appear to be too useful on the command line, once you start writing playbooks, it will come into its own.

If all the modules in Ansible do as little as the `setup` and the `ping` module, we will not be able to change anything on the remote machine. Almost all of the other modules that Ansible provides, such as the file module, allow us to actually configure the remote machine.

The file module can be called with a single path argument; this will cause it to return information about the file in question. If you give it more arguments, it will try and alter the file's attributes and tell you if it has changed anything. Ansible modules will almost always tell you if they have changed anything, which becomes more important when you are writing playbooks.

You can call the file module, as shown in the following command, to see details about `/etc/fstab`:

```
$ ansible machinename -u root -k -m file -a 'path=/etc/fstab'
```

The preceding command should elicit a response like the following code:

```
machinename | success >> {
  "changed": false,
  "group": "root",
  "mode": "0644",
  "owner": "root",
  "path": "/etc/fstab",
```

```
    "size": 779,
    "state":
    "file"

}
```

Or like the following command to create a new test directory `in /tmp`:

```
$ ansible machinename -u root -k -m file -a 'path=/tmp/test
state=directory mode=0700 owner=root'
```

The preceding command should return something like the following code:

```
machinename | success >> {
    "changed": true,
    "group": "root",
    "mode": "0700",
    "owner": "root",
    "path": "/tmp/test",
    "size": 4096,
    "state": "directory"
}
```

The second command will have the changed variable set to `true`, if the directory doesn't exist or has different attributes. When run a second time, the value of changed should be `false` indicating that no changes were required.

There are several modules that accept similar arguments to the file module, and one such example is the `copy` module. The `copy` module takes a file on the controller machine, copies it to the managed machine, and sets the attributes as required. For example, to copy the `/etc/fstab` file to `/tmp` on the managed machine, you will use the following command:

```
$ ansible machinename -m copy -a 'path=/tmp/fstab mode=0700
owner=root'
```

The preceding command, when run the first time, should return something like the following code:

```
machinename | success >> {
    "changed": true,
    "dest": "/tmp/fstab",
    "group": "root",
    "md5sum": "fe9304aa7b683f58609ec7d3ee9eea2f",
    "mode": "0700",
    "owner": "root",
```

```
    "size": 637,
    "src": "/root/.ansible/tmp/ansible-1374060150.96-
      77605185106940/source",
    "state": "file"
}
```

There is also a module called `command` that will run any arbitrary command on the managed machine. This lets you configure it with any arbitrary command, such as a preprovided installer or a self-written script; it is also useful for rebooting machines. Please note that this module does not run the command within the shell, so you cannot perform redirection, use pipes, and expand shell variables or background commands.

Ansible modules strive to prevent changes being made when they are not required. This is referred to as idempotency and can make running commands against multiple servers much faster. Unfortunately, Ansible cannot know if your command has changed anything or not, so to help it be more idempotent you have to give it some help. It can do this either via the `creates` or the `removes` argument. If you give a `creates` argument, the command will not be run if the filename argument exists. The opposite is true of the `removes` argument; if the filename exists, the command will be run.

You run the command as follows:

```
$ ansible machinename -m command -a 'rm -rf /tmp/testing
removes=/tmp/testing'
```

If there is no file or directory named `/tmp/testing`, the command output will indicate that it was skipped, as follows:

```
machinename | skipped
```

Otherwise, if the file did exist, it will look as follows:

```
ansibletest | success | rc=0 >>
```

Often it is better to use another module in place of the `command` module. Other modules offer more options and can better capture the problem domain they work in. For example, it would be much less work for Ansible and also the person writing the configurations to use the file module in this instance, since the `file` module will recursively delete something if the state is set to absent. So, this command would be equivalent to the following command:

```
$ ansible machinename -m file -a 'path=/tmp/testing state=absent'
```

If you need to use features usually available in a shell while running your command, you will need the `shell` module. This way you can use redirection, pipes, or job backgrounding. You can pick which shell to use with the executable argument. However, when you write the code, it also supports the `creates` argument but does not support the removes argument. You can use the shell module as follows:

```
$ ansible machinename -m shell -a '/opt/fancyapp/bin/installer.sh >
/var/log/fancyappinstall.log creates=/var/log/fancyappinstall.log'
```

Module help

Unfortunately, we don't have enough space to cover every module that is available in Ansible; luckily though, Ansible includes a command called `ansible-doc` that can retrieve help information. All the modules included with Ansible have this data populated; however, with modules gathered from elsewhere you may find less help. The `ansible-doc` command also allows you to see a list of all modules available to you.

To get a list of all the modules that are available to you along with a short description of each type, use the following command:

```
$ ansible-doc -l
```

To see the help file for a particular module, you supply it as the single argument to `ansible-doc`. To see the help information for the `file` module, for example, use the following command:

```
$ ansible-doc file
```

Summary

In this chapter, we have covered which installation type to choose, installing Ansible, and how to build an inventory file to reflect your environment. After this, we saw how to use Ansible modules in an ad hoc style for simple tasks. Finally, we discussed how to learn which modules are available on your system and how to use the command line to get instructions for using a module.

In the next chapter, we will learn how to use many modules together in a playbook. This allows you to perform more complex tasks than you could do with single modules alone.

2 Simple Playbooks

Ansible is useful as a command-line tool for making small changes. However, its real power lies in its scripting abilities. While setting up machines, you almost always need to do more than one thing at a time. Ansible provides for this by using a tool called playbook. Using playbooks, you can perform many actions at once, and across multiple systems. They provide a way to orchestrate deployments, ensure a consistent configuration, or simply perform a common task.

Playbooks are expressed in **YAML**, and for the most part, Ansible uses a standard YAML parser. This means that you have all the features of YAML available to you as you write them. For example, you can use the same commenting system as you would in YAML. Many lines of a playbook can also be written and represented in YAML data types. See `http://www.yaml.org/` for more information.

Playbooks also open up many opportunities. They allow you to carry the state from one command to the next. For example, you can grab the content of a file on one machine, register it as a variable, and then use that on another machine. This allows you to make complex deployment mechanisms that will be impossible with the Ansible command alone. Additionally, each module tries to be idempotent; you should be able to run a playbook several times and changes will only be made if they need to be.

The command to execute a playbook is `ansible-playbook`. It accepts arguments similar to the Ansible command-line tool. For example, `-k` (`--ask-pass`) and `-K` (`--ask-sudo`) make it prompt for the **SSH** and sudo passwords, respectively; `-u` can be used to set the user to use SSH. However, these options can also be set inside the playbooks themselves in the target section. For example, to use the play named `example-play.yml`, you can use the following command:

```
$ ansible-playbook example-play.yml
```

The Ansible playbooks are made up of one or more plays. A play consists of three sections: the target section, the variable section, and finally the bit that does all the real work, the task section. You can include as many plays as you like in a single YAML file.

- The target section defines hosts on which the play will be run, and how it will be run. This is where you set the SSH username and other SSH-related settings.
- The variable section defines variables which will be made available to the play while running.
- The task section lists all the modules in the order that you want them to be run by Ansible.

A full example of an Ansible play looks like the following code snippet:

```
---
- hosts: localhost
  user: root
  vars:
    motd_warning: 'WARNING: Use by ACME Employees ONLY'
  tasks:
    - name: setup a MOTD
      copy: dest=/etc/motd content={{ motd_warning }}
```

The target section

The target section looks like the following code snippet:

```
- hosts: webservers
  user: root
```

This is an incredibly simple version, but likely to be all you need in most cases. Each play exists within a list. As per the YAML syntax, the line must start with a dash. The hosts that a play will be run on must be set in the value of `hosts`. This value uses the same syntax as the one used when selecting hosts using the Ansible command line, which we discussed in the previous chapter. The host-pattern-matching features of Ansible were also discussed in the previous chapter. In the next line, the user tells the Ansible playbook which user to connect to the machine as.

The other lines that you can provide in this section are as follows:

Name	Description
`sudo`	Set this to `yes` if you want Ansible to use sudo to become root once it is connected to the machines in the play.
`user`	This defines the username to connect to the machine originally, before running sudo if configured.
`sudo_user`	This is the user that Ansible will try and become using sudo. For example, if you set `sudo` to `yes` and `user` to `daniel`, setting `sudo_user` to `kate` will cause Ansible to use sudo to get from `daniel` to `kate` once logged in. If you were doing this in an interactive SSH session, you will use `sudo -u kate` while you are logged in as `daniel`.
`connection`	`connection` allows you to tell Ansible what transport to use to connect to the remote host. You will mostly use `ssh` or `paramiko` for remote hosts. However, you can also use `local` to avoid a connection overhead when running things on the `localhost`. Most of the time you will be using either `local` or `ssh` here.
`gather_facts`	Ansible will automatically run the setup module on the remote hosts unless you tell it not to. If you don't need the variables from the setup module, you can set this now and save some time.

The variable section

Here you can define variables that apply to the entire play on all machines. You can also make Ansible prompt for variables if they weren't supplied in the command line. This allows you to make easily maintainable plays, and prevents you from changing the same thing in several parts of the play. This also allows you to have all the configuration for the play stored at the top, where you can easily read and modify it without worrying about what the rest of the play does.

Variables in this section of a play can be overridden by machine facts (those that are set by modules), but they themselves override the facts you set in your inventory. So they are useful to define defaults that you may collect in a module later, but they can't be used to keep defaults for inventory variables as they will override those defaults.

Variable declarations, called `vars`, look like the values in the target section and contain a YAML dictionary or a list. An example looks like the following code snippet:

```
vars:
  apache_version: 2.6
  motd_warning: 'WARNING: Use by ACME Employees ONLY'
  testserver: yes
```

Variables can also be loaded from external YAML files by giving Ansible a list of variable files to load. This is done in a similar way using the `vars_files` directive. Then simply provide the name of another YAML file that contains its own dictionary. This means that instead of storing the variables in the same file, they can be stored and distributed separately, allowing you to share your playbook with others.

Using `vars`, the files look like the following code snippet in your playbook:

```
vars_files:
  /conf/country-AU.yml
  /conf/datacenter-SYD.yml
  /conf/cluster-mysql.yml
```

In the previous example, Ansible looks for `country-AU.yml`, `datacenter-SYD.yml`, and `cluster-mysql.yml` in the `conf` folder. Each YAML file looks similar to the following code snippet:

```
---
ntp: 'ntp1.au.example.com'
TZ: 'Australia/Sydney'
```

Finally you can make Ansible ask the user for each variable interactively. This is useful when you have variables that you don't want to make available for automation, and instead require human input. One example where this is useful is prompting for the passphrases used to decrypt secret keys for the HTTPS servers.

You can instruct Ansible to prompt for variables with the following code snippet:

```
vars_prompt:
  - name: 'https_passphrase'
    prompt: 'Key Passphrase'
    private: yes
```

In the previous example, `https_passphrase` is where the entered data will be stored. The user will be prompted with `Key Passphrase`, and because `private` is set to `yes`, the value will not be printed on the screen as the user enters it.

You can use variables, facts, and inventory variables with the help of: `{{ variablename }}`, `${variablename}`, or simply `$variablename`. You can even refer to complex variables, such as dictionaries, with a dotted notation. For example, a variable named `httpd`, with a key in it called `maxclients`, will be accessed as `{{ httpd.maxclients }}`. This works with facts from the setup module too. For example, you can get the IPv4 address of a network interface called eth0 using `{{ ansible_eth0.ipv4.address }}`.

Variables that are set in the variable section do not survive between different plays in the same playbook. However, facts gathered by the setup module or set by `set_fact` do. This means that if you are running a second play on the same machines, or a subset of the machines in an earlier play, you can set `gather_facts` in the target section to `false`. The setup module can sometimes take a while to run, so this can dramatically speed up plays, especially in plays where the serial is set to a low value.

The task section

The task section is the last section of each play. It contains a list of the actions that you want Ansible to perform in the order you want them to be performed. There are several ways in which you can represent each module's configuration. We suggest you try to stick with one as much as possible, and use the others only when required. This makes your playbooks easier to read and maintain. The following code snippet is what a task section looks like with all three styles shown:

```
tasks:
  - name: install apache
    action: yum name=httpd state=installed

  - name: configure apache
    copy: src=files/httpd.conf dest=/etc/httpd/conf/httpd.conf

  - name: restart apache
    service:
      name: httpd
      state: restarted
```

Here we see the three different styles being used to install, configure, and start the Apache web server as it will look on a CentOS machine. The first task shows you how to install Apache using the original syntax, which requires you to call the module as the first keyword inside an `action` key. The second task copies Apache's configuration file into place using the second style of the task. In this style, you use the module name in place of the `action` keyword and its value simply becomes its argument. This form is the one recommended by the Ansible authors. Finally the last task, the third style, shows how to use the service module to restart Apache. In this style, you use the module name as the key, as usual, but you also supply the arguments as a YAML dictionary. This can come in handy when you are providing a large number of arguments to a single module, or if the module wants the arguments in a complex form, such as the Cloud Formation module.

Note that names are not required for tasks. However, they make good documentation and allow you to refer to each task later on if required. This will become useful especially when we come to handlers. The names are also outputted to the console when the playbook is run, so that the user can tell what is happening. If you don't provide a name, Ansible will just use the action line of the task or the handler.

> Unlike other configuration management tools, Ansible does not provide a fully featured dependency system. This is a blessing and a curse; with a complete dependency system, you can get to a point where you are never quite sure what changes will be applied to particular machines. Ansible, however, does guarantee that your changes will be executed in the order they are written. So, if one module depends on another module that is executed before it, simply place one before the other in the playbook.

The handlers section

The handlers section is syntactically the same as the task section and supports the same format for calling modules. The modules in the handlers section are not run unless they are called by tasks. They are called only when the task they were called from records that they changed something. You simply add a notify key to the task with the value set to the name of the task.

Handlers are run when Ansible has finished running the task list. They are run in the order that they are listed in the handlers section, and even if they are called multiple times in the task section, they will run only once. This is often used to restart daemons after they have been upgraded and configured. The following play demonstrates how you will upgrade an ISC DHCP server to the latest version, configure it, and set it to start at boot. If this playbook is run on a server where the ISC DHCP daemon is already running the latest version and the config files are not changed, the handler will not be called and DHCP will not be restarted.

```
---
- hosts: dhcp
  tasks:
  - name: update to latest DHCP
    action: yum name=dhcp state=latest
    notify: restart dhcp

  - name: copy the DHCP config
    action: copy src=dhcp/dhcpd.conf dest=/etc/dhcp/dhcpd.conf
    notify: restart dhcp

  - name: start DHCP at boot
    action: service name=dhcpd state=started enabled=yes

  handlers:
  - name: restart dhcp
    action: service name=dhcpd state=restarted
```

Each handler can only be a single module, but you can notify a list of handlers from a single task. This allows you to trigger many handlers from a single step in the task list. For example, if you have just checked out a new version of a Django application, you might set a handler to migrate the database, deploy the static files, and restart Apache. You can do this by simply using a YAML list on the notify action. This might look something like the following code snippet:

```
---
- hosts: qroud
  tasks:
  - name: checkout Qroud
    action: git repo=git@github.com:smarthall/Qroud.git
      dest=/opt/apps/Qroud force=no
    notify:
      - migrate db
      - generate static
      - restart httpd

  handlers:
  - name: migrate db
    action: command chdir=/opt/apps/Qroud ./manage.py migrate -all

  - name: generate static
    action: command chdir=/opt/apps/Qroud ./manage.py
      collectstatic -c -noinput

  - name: restart httpd
    action: service name=httpd state=restarted
```

You can see that the `git` module is used to check out some public GitHub code, and if that caused anything to change, it triggers the `migrate db`, `generate static`, and `restart httpd` actions.

The playbook modules

Using modules in playbooks is a little bit different from using them in the command line. This is mainly because we have many facts available from the previous modules and the setup module. Certain modules don't work in the Ansible command line because they require access to those variables. Other modules will work in the command-line version, but are able to provide enhanced functionalities when used in a playbook.

The template module

One of the most frequently used examples of a module that requires facts from Ansible is the `template` module. This module allows you to design an outline of a configuration file and then have Ansible insert values in the right places. In reality, the Jinja2 templates can be much more complicated than this, including things such as conditionals, for loops, and macros. The following is an example of a Jinja2 configuration file for configuring BIND:

```
# {{ ansible_managed }}
options {
  listen-on port 53 {
    127.0.0.1;
    {% for ip in ansible_all_ipv4_addresses %}
      {{ ip }};
    {% endfor %}
  };
  listen-on-v6 port 53 { ::1; };
  directory       "/var/named";
  dump-file       "/var/named/data/cache_dump.db";
  statistics-file "/var/named/data/named_stats.txt";
  memstatistics-file "/var/named/data/named_mem_stats.txt";
};

zone "." IN {
  type hint;
  file "named.ca";
};

include "/etc/named.rfc1912.zones";
```

```
include "/etc/named.root.key";

{# Variables for zone config #}
{% if 'authorativenames' in group_names %}
  {% set zone_type = 'master' %}
  {% set zone_dir = 'data' %}
{% else %}
  {% set zone_type = 'slave' %}
  {% set zone_dir = 'slaves' %}
{% endif %}

zone "internal.example.com" IN {
  type {{ zone_type }};
  file "{{ zone_dir }}/internal.example.com";
  {% if 'authorativenames' not in group_names %}
    masters { 192.168.2.2; };
  {% endif %}
};
```

The first line merely sets up a comment that shows which template the file came from, the host, modification time of the template, and the owner. Putting this somewhere in the template as a comment is a good practice, and it ensures that people know what they should edit if they wish to alter it permanently. In the fifth line, there is a `for` loop. For loops go through all the elements of a list once for each item in the list. It optionally assigns the item to the variable of your choice so that you can use it inside the loop. This one loops across all the values in `ansible_all_ipv4_addresses`, which is a list from the setup module that contains all the IPv4 addresses that the machine has. Inside the for loop, it simply adds each of them into the configuration to make sure BIND will listen on that interface.

Line 24 of the preceding code snippet has a comment. Anything in between `{#` and `#}` is simply ignored by the Jinja2 template processor. This allows you to add comments in the template that do not make it into the final file. This is especially handy if you are doing something complicated, setting variables within the template, or if the configuration file does not allow comments.

In the very next line we can see an `if` statement. Anything between `{% if %}` and `{% endif %}` is ignored if the statement in the `if` tag is false. Here we check if the value `authorativenames` is in the list of group names that apply to this host. If this is true, the next two lines set two custom variables. `zone_type` is set to master and `zone_dir` is set to data. If this host is not in the `authorativenames` group, `zone_type` and `zone_dir` will be set to `slave` and `slaves`, respectively.

In line 33, we start the configuration of the zone. We set the type to the variable we created earlier, and the location to `zone_dir`. Finally we check again if the host is in the `authorativenames` groups, and if it isn't, we configure its master to a particular IP address.

To get this template to set up an authorative nameserver, you need to create a group in your inventory file named `authorativenames` and add some hosts under it. How to do this was discussed back in *Chapter 1, Getting Started with Ansible*.

You can simply call the `templates` module and the facts from the machines will be sent through, including the groups the machine is in. This is as simple as calling any other module. The `template` module also accepts similar arguments to the copy module such as owner, group, and mode.

```
---
- name: Setup BIND
  host: allnames
  tasks:
  - name: configure BIND
    template: src=templates/named.conf.j2 dest=/etc/named.conf
      owner=root group=named mode=0640
```

The set_fact module

The `set_fact` module allows you to build your own facts on the machine inside an Ansible play. These facts can then be used inside templates or as variables in the playbook. Facts act just like arguments that come from modules such as the setup module: in that they work on a per-host basis. You should use this to avoid putting complex logic into templates. For example, if you are trying to configure a buffer to take a certain percentage of RAM, you should calculate the value in the playbook.

The following example shows how to use `set_fact` to configure a MySQL server to have an InnoDB buffer size of approximately half of the total RAM available on the machine:

```
---     #1
- name: Configure MySQL      #2
  hosts: mysqlservers      #3
  tasks:      #4
  - name: install MySql      #5
    yum: name=mysql-server state=installed      #6

  - name: Calculate InnoDB buffer pool size      #7
    set_fact: innodb_buffer_pool_size_mb="{{ ansible_memtotal_mb /
      2 }}"     #8
```

```
- name: Configure MySQL     #9
  template: src=templates/my.cnf.j2 dest=/etc/my.cnf owner=root
    group=root mode=0644     #10
  notify: restart mysql     #11

- name: Start MySQL     #12
  service: name=mysqld state=started enabled=yes     #13

handlers:     #14
- name: restart mysql     #15
  service: name=mysqld state=restarted     #16
```

The first task here simply installs MySQL using yum. The second task creates a fact by getting the total memory of the managed machine, dividing it by two, losing any non-integer remainder, and putting it in a fact called `innodb_buffer_pool_size_mb`. The next line then loads a template into `/etc/my.cnf` to configure MySQL. Finally, MySQL is started and set to start at boot time. A handler is also included to restart MySQL when its configuration changes.

The template then only needs to get the value of `innodb_buffer_pool_size` and place it into the configuration. This means that you can re-use the same template in places where the buffer pool should be one-fifth of the RAM, or one-eighth, and simply change the playbook for those hosts. In this case, the template will look something like the following code snippet:

```
# {{ ansible_managed }}
[mysqld]
datadir=/var/lib/mysql
socket=/var/lib/mysql/mysql.sock
# Disabling symbolic-links is recommended to prevent assorted
  security risks
symbolic-links=0
# Settings user and group are ignored when systemd is used.
# If you need to run mysqld under a different user or group,
# customize your systemd unit file for mysqld according to the
# instructions in http://fedoraproject.org/wiki/Systemd

# Configure the buffer pool
innodb_buffer_pool_size = {{
  innodb_buffer_pool_size_mb|default(128) }}M

[mysqld_safe]
log-error=/var/log/mysqld.log
pid-file=/var/run/mysqld/mysqld.pid
```

You can see that in the previous template, we are simply putting the variables we get from the play into the template. If the template doesn't see the `innodb_buffer_pool_size_mb` fact, it simply uses a default of 128.

The pause module

The `pause` module stops the execution of a playbook for a certain period of time. You can configure it to wait for a particular period, or you can make it prompt the user to continue. While effectively useless when used from the Ansible command line, it can be very handy when used inside a playbook.

Generally, the `pause` module is used when you want the user to provide confirmation to continue, or if manual intervention is required at a particular point. For example, if you have just deployed a new version of a web application to a server, and you need to have the user check manually to make sure it looks okay before you configure them to receive production traffic, you can put a pause there. It is also handy to warn the user of a possible problem and give them the option of continuing. This will make Ansible print out the names of the servers and ask the user to press *Enter* to continue. If used with the serial key in the target section, it will ask once for each group of hosts that Ansible is running on. This way you can give the user the flexibility of running the deployment at their own pace while they interactively monitor the progress.

Less usefully, this module can simply wait for a specified period of time. This is often not useful as you usually don't know how long a particular action may take, and guessing may have disastrous outcomes. You should not use it for waiting for networked daemons to start up; you should use the `wait_for` module (described in the next section) for this task. The following play demonstrates using the `pause` module first in the user interactive mode and then in the timed mode:

```
---
- hosts: localhost
  tasks:
  - name: wait on user input
    pause: prompt="Warning! Detected slight issue. ENTER to
      continue CTRL-C a to quit."

  - name: timed wait
    pause: seconds=30
```

The wait_for module

The `wait_for` module is used to poll a particular TCP port and not continue until that port accepts a remote connection. The polling is done from the remote machine. If you only provide a port, or set the host argument to `localhost`, the poll will try to connect to the managed machine. You can utilize `local_action` to run the command from the controller machine and use the `ansible_hostname` variable as your host argument to make it try and connect to the managed machine from the controller machine.

This module is particularly useful for daemons that can take a while to start, or things that you want to run in the background. Apache Tomcat ships with an init script that when you try to start it immediately returns, leaving Tomcat starting in the background. Depending on the application that Tomcat is configured to load, it might take anywhere between two seconds to 10 minutes to fully start up and be ready for connections. You can time your application's start up and use the `pause` module. However, the next deployment may take longer or shorter, and this can break your deployment mechanism. With the `wait_for` module, you have Ansible to recognize when Tomcat is ready to accept connections. The following is a play that does exactly this:

```
---
- hosts: webapps
  tasks:
  - name: Install Tomcat
    yum: name=tomcat7 state=installed

  - name: Start Tomcat
    service: name=tomcat7 state=started

  - name: Wait for Tomcat to start
    wait_for: port=8080 state=started
```

After the completion of this play, Tomcat should be installed, started, and ready to accept requests. You can append further modules to this example and depend on Tomcat being available and listening.

The assemble module

The `assemble` module combines several files on the managed machine and saves them to another file on the managed machine. This is useful in playbooks when you have a `config` file that does not allow includes, or globbing in its includes. This is useful for the `authorized_keys` file for say, the root user. The following play will send a bunch of SSH public keys to the managed machine, then make it assemble them all together and place it in the root user's home directory:

```
---     #1
- hosts: all      #2
  tasks:      #3
  - name: Make a Directory in /opt      #4
    file: path=/opt/sshkeys state=directory owner=root group=root
      mode=0700      #5

  - name: Copy SSH keys over      #6
    copy: src=keys/{{ item }}.pub dest=/opt/sshkeys/{{ item }}.pub
      owner=root group=root mode=0600      #7
    with_items:      #8
      - dan      #9
      - kate      #10
      - mal      #11

  - name: Make the root users SSH config directory      #12
    file: path=/root/.ssh state=directory owner=root group=root
      mode=0700      #13

  - name: Build the authorized_keys file      #14
    assemble: src=/opt/sshkeys dest=/root/.ssh/authorized_keys
      owner=root group=root mode=0700      #15
```

By now this should all look familiar. You may note the `with_items` key in the task that copies the keys over, and the `{{ items }}` variable. These will be explained later in *Chapter 3, Advanced Playbooks*, but all you need to know now is that whatever item you supply to the `with_items` key is substituted into the `{{ items }}` variable, similar to how a for loop works. This simply lets us easily copy many files to the remote host at once.

The last task shows the usage of the `assemble` module. You pass the directory containing the files to be concatenated into the output as the `src` argument, and then pass `dest` as the output file. It also accepts many of the same arguments (`owner`, `group`, and `mode`) as the other modules that create files. It also combines the files in the same order as the `ls -1` command lists them. This means you can use the same approach as `udev` and `rc.d`, and prepend numbers to the files to ensure that they end up in the correct order.

The add_host module

The `add_host` module is one of the most powerful modules that is available in playbooks. `add_host` lets you dynamically add new machines inside a play. You can do this by using the `uri` module to get a host from your CMDB and then adding it to the current play. This module will also add your host to a group, dynamically creating that group if it does not already exist.

The module simply takes a `hostname` and a `groups` argument, which are rather self-explanatory, and sets the hostname and groups. You can also send extra arguments and these are treated in the same way in which extra values in the inventory file are treated. This means you can set `ansible_ssh_user`, `ansible_ssh_port`, and so on.

The group_by module

In addition to creating hosts dynamically in your play, you can also create groups. The `group_by` module can create groups based on the facts about the machines, including the ones you set up yourself using the `add_fact` module explained earlier. The `group_by` module accepts one argument, `key`, which takes the name of a group the machine will be added to. Combining this with the use of variables, you can make the module add a server to a group based on its operating system, visualization technology, or any other fact that you have access to. You can then use this group in the target section of any subsequent plays, or in templates.

So if you want to create a group that groups the hosts by operating system, you will call the module as follows. You can then use these groups to install packages using the right packager, for example:

```
---
- name: Create operating system group
  hosts: all
  tasks:
    - group_by: key=os_{{ ansible_distribution }}

- name: Run on CentOS hosts only
  hosts: os_CentOS
  tasks:
  - name: Install Apache
    yum: name=httpd state=latest

- name: Run on Ubuntu hosts only
  hosts: os_Ubuntu
  tasks:
  - name: Install Apache
    apt: pkg=apache2 state=latest
```

Summary

In this chapter, we covered the sections that are available in the playbook file, how you can use variables to make your playbooks maintainable, triggering handlers when changes have been made, and finally we looked at how certain modules are more useful when used inside a playbook.

In the next chapter, we will be looking into the more complex features of playbooks. This will allow you to build more complex playbooks capable of deploying and configuring entire systems.

3
Advanced Playbooks

So far the playbooks that we have looked at are simple and just run a number of modules in order. Ansible allows much more control over the execution of your playbook. Using the following techniques, you should be able to perform even the most complex deployments.

Running operations in parallel

By default, Ansible will only fork up to five times, so it will only run an operation on five different machines at once. If you have a large number of machines, or you have lowered this maximum fork value, then you may want to launch things asynchronously. Ansible's method for doing this is to launch the task and then poll for it to complete. This allows Ansible to start the job across all the required machines while still using the maximum forks.

To run an operation in parallel, use the `async` and `poll` keywords. The `async` keyword triggers Ansible to run the job in parallel, and its value will be the maximum time that Ansible will wait for the command to complete. The value of `poll` indicates to Ansible how often to poll to check if the command has been completed.

If you wanted to run `updatedb` across an entire cluster of machines, it might look like the following code:

```
- hosts: all
  tasks:
    - name: Install mlocate
      yum: name=mlocate state=installed
```

```
- name: Run updatedb
  command: /usr/bin/updatedb
  async: 300
  poll: 10
```

You will notice that when you run the previous example on more than five machines, the `yum` module acts differently to the `command` module. The `yum` module will run on the first five machines, then the next five, and so on. The `command` module, however, will run across all the machines and indicate the status once complete.

If your command starts a daemon that eventually listens on a port, you can start it without polling so that Ansible does not check for it to complete. You can then carry on with other actions and check for completion later using the `wait_for` module. To configure Ansible to not wait for the job to complete, set the value of `poll` to `0`.

Finally, if the task that you are running takes an extremely long time to run, you can tell Ansible to wait for the job as long as it takes. To do this, set the value of `async` to `0`.

You will want to use Ansible's polling in the following situations:

- You have a long-running task that may hit the timeout
- You need to run an operation across a large number of machines
- You have an operation for which you don't need to wait to complete

There are also a few situations where you should not use `async` or `poll`:

- If your job acquires locks that prevent other things from running
- You job only takes a short time to run

Looping

Ansible allows you to repeat a module several times with different input, for example, if you had several files that should have similar permissions set. This can save you a lot of repetition and allows you to iterate over facts and variables.

To do this, you can use the `with_items` key on an action and set the value to the list of items that you are going to iterate over. This will create a variable for the module called `item`, which will be set to each item in turn as your module is iterated over. Some modules such as `yum` will optimize this so that instead of doing a separate transaction for each package, they will operate on all of them at once.

Using `with_items` looks like this:

```
tasks:
 - name: Secure config files
   file: path=/etc/{{ item }} mode=0600 owner=root group=root
   with_items:
    - my.cnf
    - shadow
    - fstab
```

In addition to looping over fixed items, or a variable, Ansible can also use what are called **lookup plugins**. These plugins allow you to tell Ansible to fetch the data from somewhere externally. For example, you might want to upload all the files that match a particular pattern, and then upload them.

In this example, we upload all the public keys in a directory and then assemble them into an `authorized_keys` file for the root user.

```
tasks:     #1
 - name: Make key directory     #2
   file: path=/root/.sshkeys ensure=directory mode=0700
    owner=root group=root     #3

 - name: Upload public keys     #4
   copy: src={{ item }} dest=/root/.sshkeys mode=0600
    owner=root group=root     #5
   with_fileglob:     #6
    - keys/*.pub     #7

 - name: Assemble keys into authorized_keys file     #8
   assemble: src=/root/.sshkeys dest=/root/.ssh/authorized_keys
    mode=0600 owner=root group=root     #9
```

Repeating modules can be used in the following situations:

- Repeating a module many times with similar settings
- Iterating over all the values of a fact that is a list
- Used to create many files for later use with the `assemble` module to combine into one large file
- Used `with_fileglob` to copy a directory of files using the glob pattern matching

Conditional execution

Some modules, such as the `copy` module, provide mechanisms to configure it to skip the module. You can also configure your own skip conditions that will only execute the module if they resolve to `true`. This can be handy if your servers use different packaging systems or have different filesystem layouts. It can also be used with the `set_fact` module to allow you to compute many different things.

To skip a module, you can use the `when` key; this lets you provide a condition. If the condition you set resolves to `false`, then the module will be skipped. The value that you assign to `when` is a Python expression. You can use any of the variables or facts available to you at this point.

If you only want to process some of the items in the list depending on a condition, then simply use the `when` clause. The `when` clause is processed separately for each item in the list; the item being processed is available as a variable using `{{ item }}`.

The following code is an example showing how to choose between `apt` and `yum` for both Debian and Red Hat systems. There is also a third clause to print a message and fail if the OS is not recognized.

```
---     #1
- name: Install VIM     #2
  hosts: all     #3
  tasks:     #4
    - name: Install VIM via yum     #5
      yum: name=vim-enhanced state=installed     #6
      when: ansible_os_family == "RedHat"     #7

    - name: Install VIM via apt     #8
      apt: name=vim state=installed     #9
      when: ansible_os_family == "Debian"     #10

    - name: Unexpected OS family     #11
      debug: msg="OS Family {{ ansible_os_family }} is not
        supported" fail=yes     #12
      when: not ansible_os_family == "RedHat" or ansible_os_family
        == "Debian"     #13
```

This feature can be used to pause at a particular point and wait for the user intervention to continue. Normally when Ansible encounters an error, it will simply stop what it is doing without running any handlers. With this feature, you can add the `pause` module with a condition on it that triggers in unexpected situations. This way the `pause` module will be ignored in a normal situation, but in unexpected circumstances it will allow the user to intervene and continue when it is safe to do so.
The task would look like this:

```
name: pause for unexpected conditions
pause: prompt="Unexpected OS"
when: ansible_os_family != "RedHat"
```

There are numerous uses of skipping actions; here are a few suggestions:

- Working around differences in operating systems
- Prompting a user and only then performing actions that they request
- Improving performance by avoiding a module that you know won't change anything but may take a while to do so
- Refusing to alter systems that have a particular file present
- Checking if custom written scripts have already been run

Task delegation

Ansible, by default, runs its tasks all at once on the configured machine. This is great when you have a whole bunch of separate machines to configure, or if each of your machines is responsible for communicating its status to the other remote machines. However, if you need to perform an action on a different host than the one Ansible is operating on, you can use a delegation.

Ansible can be configured to run a task on a different host than the one that is being configured using the `delegate_to` key. The module will still run once for every machine, but instead of running on the target machine, it will run on the delegated host. The facts available will be the ones applicable to the current host. Here, we show a playbook that will use the `get_url` option to download the configuration from a bunch of web servers.

```
---     #1
- name: Fetch configuration from all webservers      #2
  hosts: webservers     #3
  tasks:      #4
    - name: Get config     #5
```

```
        get_url: dest=configs/{{ ansible_hostname }} force=yes
          url=http://{{ ansible_hostname }}/diagnostic/config     #6
        delegate_to: localhost     #7
```

If you are delegating to the `localhost`, you can use a shortcut when defining the action that automatically uses the local machine. If you define the key of the action line as `local_action`, then the delegation to `localhost` is implied. If we were to have used this in the previous example, it would be slightly shorter and look like this:

```
---     #1
- name: Fetch configuration from all webservers     #2
  hosts: webservers     #3
  tasks:     #4
    - name: Get config     #5
      local_action: get_url dest=configs/{{ ansible_hostname
        }}.cfg url=http://{{ ansible_hostname
          }}/diagnostic/config     #6
```

Delegation is not limited to the local machine. You can delegate to any host that is in the inventory. Some other reasons why you might want to delegate are:

- Removing a host from a load balancer before deployment
- Changing DNS to direct traffic away from a server you are about to change
- Creating an iSCSI volume on a storage device
- Using an external server to check that access outside the network works

Extra variables

You may have seen in our template example in the previous chapter that we used a variable called `group_names`. This is one of the magic variables that are provided by Ansible itself. At the time of writing there are seven such variables, described in the following sections.

The hostvars variable

`hostvars` allows you to retrieve variables about all the hosts that the current play has dealt with. If the setup module hasn't yet been run on that host in the current play, only its variables will be available. You can access it like you would access other complex variables, such as `${hostvars.hostname.fact}`, so to get the Linux distribution running on a server named `ns1`, it would be `${hostvars.ns1.ansible_distribution}`. The following example sets a variable called zone master to the server named `ns1`. It then calls the `template` module, which would use this to set the masters for each zone.

```
---     #1
- name: Setup DNS Servers     #2
  hosts: allnameservers     #3
  tasks:     #4
    - name: Install BIND     #5
      yum: name=named state=installed     #6

- name: Setup Slaves     #7
  hosts: slavenamesservers     #8
  tasks:     #9
    - name: Get the masters IP     #10
      set_fact: dns_master="{{
        hostvars.ns1.ansible_default_ipv4.address }}"     #11

    - name: Configure BIND     #12
      template: dest=/etc/named.conf
        src/templates/named.conf.j2     #13
```

> Using `hostvars`, you can further abstract templates from your environment. If you nest your variable calls, then instead of placing an IP address in the variable section of the play, you can add the hostname. To find the address of a machine named in the variable `the_machine` you would use, `{{ hostvars.[the_machine].default_ipv4.address }}`.

The groups variable

The `groups` variable contains a list of all hosts in the inventory grouped by the inventory group. This lets you get access to all the hosts that you have configured. This is potentially a very powerful tool. It allows you to iterate across a whole group and for every host apply an action to the current machine.

```
---     #1
- name: Configure the database     #2
  hosts: dbservers     #3
  user: root     #4
  tasks:     #5
    - name: Install mysql     #6
      yum: name={{ item }} state=installed     #7
      with_items:     #8
      - mysql-server     #9
      - MySQL-python     #10
```

```
    - name: Start mysql      #11
      service: name=mysqld state=started enabled=true      #12


    - name: Create a user for all app servers      #13
      with_items: groups.appservers      #14
      mysql_user: name=kate password=test host={{
        hostvars.[item].ansible_eth0.ipv4.address }}
          state=present      #15
```

The `groups` variable does not contain the actual hosts in the group; it contains strings representing their names in the inventory. This means you have to use nested variable expansion to get to the `hostvars` variable if needed.

You can even use this variable to create `known_hosts` files for all of your machines containing the `host` keys of all the other machines. This would allow you to then SSH from one machine to another without confirming the identity of the remote host. It would also handle removing machines when they leave service or updating them when they are replaced. The following is a template for a `known_hosts` file that does this:

```
{% for host in groups['all'] %}
{{ hostvars[host]['ansible_hostname'] }}        {{
  hostvars[host]['ansible_ssh_host_key_rsa_public'] }}
{% endfor %}
```

The playbook that uses this template would look like this:

```
---      #1
hosts: all      #2
tasks:      #3
- name: Setup known hosts      #4
  hosts: all      #5
  tasks:      #6
    - name: Create known_hosts      #7
      template: src=templates/known_hosts.j2
        dest=/etc/ssh/ssh_known_hosts owner=root group=root
          mode=0644      #8
```

The group_names variable

The `group_names` variable contains a list of strings with the names of all the groups the current host is in. This is not only useful for debugging, but also for conditionals detecting group membership. This was used in the last chapter to set up a nameserver.

This variable is mostly useful for skipping a task or in a template as a condition. For instance, if you had two configurations for the SSH daemon, one secure and one less secure, but you only wanted the secure configuration on the machines in the secure group, you would do it like this:

```
- name: Setup SSH
  hosts: sshservers
  tasks:
    - name: For secure machines
      set_fact: sshconfig=files/ssh/sshd_config_secure
      when: "'secure' in group_names"

    - name: For non-secure machines
      set_fact: sshconfig=files/ssh/sshd_config_default
      when: "'secure' not in group_names"

    - name: Copy over the config
      copy: src={{ sshconfig }} dest=/tmp/sshd_config
```

In the previous example, we used the `set_fact` module to set the fact for each case, and then used the `copy` module. We could have used the `copy` module in place of the `set_facts` modules and used one fewer task. The reason this was done is that the `set_fact` module runs locally and the `copy` module runs remotely. When you use the `set_facts` module first and only call the `copy` module once, the copies are made on all the machines in parallel. If you used two `copy` modules with conditions, then each would execute on the relevant machines separately. Since `copy` is the longer task of the two, it benefits the most from running in parallel.

The inventory_hostname variable

The `inventory_hostname` variable stores the hostname of the server as recorded in the inventory. You should use this if you have chosen not to run the setup module on the current host, or if for various reasons the value detected by the setup module is not correct. This is useful when you are doing the initial setup of the machine and changing the hostname.

The inventory_hostname_short variable

The `inventory_hostname_short` variable is the same as the previous variable; however, it only includes the characters up to the first dot. So for `host.example.com`, it would return `host`.

The inventory_dir variable

The `inventory_dir` variable is the path name of the directory containing the inventory file.

The inventory_file variable

The `inventory_file` variable is the same as the previous one, except it also includes the filename.

Finding files with variables

All modules can take variables as part of their arguments by dereferencing them with `{{` and `}}`. You can use this to load a particular file based on a variable. For example, you might want to select a different `config` file for NRPE (a Nagios check daemon) based on the architecture in use. Here is how that would look:

```
---      #1
- name: Configure NRPE for the right architecture      #2
  hosts: ansibletest      #3
  user: root      #4
  tasks:      #5
    - name: Copy in the correct NRPE config file      #6
      copy: src=files/nrpe.{{ ansible_architecture }}.conf
        dest=/etc/nagios/nrpe.cfg      #7
```

In the `copy` and the `template` modules, you can also configure Ansible to look for a set of files, and it finds them using the first one. This lets you configure a file to look for; if that file is not found a second will be used, and so on until the end of the list is reached. If the file is not found, then the module will fail. The feature is triggered by using the `first_available_file` key, and referencing `{{ item }}` in the action. The following code is an example of this feature:

```
---      #1
- name: Install an Apache config file      #2
  hosts: ansibletest      #3
  user: root      #4
  tasks:      #5
   - name: Get the best match for the machine      #6
     copy: dest=/etc/apache.conf src={{ item }}      #7
     first_available_file:      #8
      - files/apache/{{ ansible_os_family }}-{{
        ansible_architecture }}.cfg      #9
      - files/apache/default-{{ ansible_architecture }}.cfg      #10
      - files/apache/default.cfg      #11
```

> Remember that you can run the setup module from the Ansible command-line tool. This comes in handy when you are making heavy use of variables in your playbooks or templates. To check what facts will be available for a particular play, simply copy the value of the host line and run the following command:
>
> `ansible [host line] -m setup`

On a CentOS x86_64 machine, this configuration would first look for the file `RedHat-x86_64.cfg` upon navigating through `files/apache/`. If that file did not exist, it would look for file `default-x86_64.cfg` upon navigating through `file/apache/`, and finally if nothing exists, it'll try and use `default.cfg`.

Environment variables

Often Unix commands take advantage of certain environment variables. Prevalent examples of this are C makefiles, installers, and the AWS command-line tools. Fortunately, Ansible makes this really easy. If you wanted to upload a file on the remote machine to Amazon S3, you could set the Amazon access key as follows. You will also see that we install EPEL so that we can install pip, and pip is used to install the AWS tools.

```
---      #1
- name: Upload a remote file via S3      #2
  hosts: ansibletest      #3
  user: root      #4
  tasks:      #5
    - name: Setup EPEL      #6
      command rpm -ivh      #7
        http://download.fedoraproject.org/pub/epel/6/i386/epel-
          release-6-8.noarch.rpm
            creates=/etc/yum.repos.d/epel.repo      #8

    - name: Install pip      #9
      yum: name=python-pip state=installed      #10

    - name: Install the AWS tools      #11
      pip: name=awscli state=present      #12

    - name: Upload the file      #13
      shell: aws s3 put-object --bucket=my-test-bucket --key={{
        ansible_hostname }}/fstab --body=/etc/fstab --region=eu-
          west-1      #14
      environment:      #15
        AWS_ACCESS_KEY_ID: XXXXXXXXXXXXXXXXXXX      #16
        AWS_SECRET_ACCESS_KEY: XXXXXXXXXXXXXXXXXXXXX      #17
```

> Internally, Ansible sets the environment variable into the Python code; this means that any module that already uses environment variables can take advantage of the ones set here. If you write your own modules, you should consider if certain arguments would be better used as environment variables instead of arguments.

Some Ansible modules such as `get_url`, `yum`, and `apt` will also use environment variables to set their proxy server. Some of the other situations where you might want to set environment variables are as follows:

- Running application installers
- Adding extra items to the path when using the `shell` module
- Loading libraries from a place not included in the system library search path
- Using an `LD_PRELOAD` hack while running a module

External data lookups

Ansible introduced the lookup plugins in Version 0.9. These plugins allow Ansible to fetch data from outside sources. Ansible provides several plugins, but you can also write your own. This really opens the doors and allows you to be flexible in your configuration.

Lookup plugins are written in Python and run on the controlling machine. They are executed in two different ways: direct calls and `with_*` keys. Direct calls are useful when you want to use them like you would use variables. Using the `with_*` keys is useful when you want to use them as loops. In an earlier section we covered `with_fileglob`, which is an example of this.

In the next example, we use a lookup plugin directly to get the `http_proxy` value from `environment` and send it through to the configured machine. This makes sure that the machines we are configuring will use the same proxy server to download the file.

```
---      #1
- name: Downloads a file using the same proxy as the controlling
    machine      #2
  hosts: all      #3
  tasks:      #4
    - name: Download file      #5
      get_url: dest=/var/tmp/file.tar.gz
        url=http://server/file.tar.gz      #6
      environment:      #7
        http_proxy: "{{ lookup('env', 'http_proxy') }}"      #8
```

You can also use lookup plugins in the variable section too. This doesn't immediately lookup the result and put it in the variable as you might assume; instead, it stores it as a macro and looks it up every time you use it. This is good to know if you are using something the value of which might change over time.

Using lookup plugins in the `with_*` form will allow you to iterate over things you wouldn't normally be able to. You can use any plugin like this, but ones that return a list are most useful. In the following code, we show how to dynamically register a `webapp` farm. If you were using this example, you would append a task to create each as a virtual machine and then a new play to configure each of them.

```
---
- name: Registers the app server farm
  hosts: localhost
  connection: local
  vars:
    hostcount: 5
  tasks:
   - name: Register the webapp farm
     local_action: add_host name={{ item }} groupname=webapp
     with_sequence: start=1 end={{ hostcount }} format=webapp%02x
```

Situations where lookup plugins are useful are as follows:

- Copying a whole directory of apache config to a conf.d style directory
- Using environment variables to adjust what the playbooks does
- Getting configuration from DNS TXT records
- Fetching the output of a command into a variable

Storing results

Almost every module outputs something, even the `debug` module. Most of the time the only variable used is the one named `changed`. The `changed` variable helps Ansible decide whether to run handlers or not and which color to print the output in. However, if you wish you can store the returned values and use them later in the playbook. In this example we look at the mode in the `/tmp` directory and create a new directory called `/tmp/subtmp` with the same mode.

```
---
- name: Using register
  hosts: ansibletest
  user: root
```

```
tasks:
  - name: Get /tmp info
    file: dest=/tmp state=directory
    register: tmp

  - name: Set mode on /var/tmp
    file: dest=/tmp/subtmp mode={{ tmp.mode }} state=directory
```

Some modules, like we see in the previous file module, can be configured to simply give information. Combining this with the register feature, you can create playbooks that can examine the environment and calculate how to proceed.

Combining the register feature and the `set_fact` module allows you to perform data processing on data you receive back from modules. This allows you to compute values and perform data processing on these values. This makes your playbooks even smarter and more flexible than ever.

Register allows you to make your own facts about hosts from modules already available to you. This can be useful in many different circumstances:

- Getting a list of files in a remote directory and downloading them all with fetch
- Running a task when a previous task changes, before the handlers run
- Getting the contents of the remote host SSH key and building a `known_hosts` file

Debugging playbooks

There are a few ways in which you can debug a playbook. Ansible includes both a verbose mode, and a debug module specifically for debugging. You can also use modules such as `fetch` and `get_url` for help. These debugging techniques can also be used to examine how modules behave when you wish to learn how to use them.

The debug module

Using the `debug` module is really quite simple. It takes two optional arguments, `msg` and `fail`. `msg` sets the message that will be printed by the module and `fail`, if set to `yes`, indicates a failure to Ansible, which will cause it to stop processing the playbook for that host. We used this module earlier in the skipping modules section to bail out of a playbook if the operating system was not recognized.

In the following example, we will show how to use the `debug` module to list all the interfaces available on the machine:

```
---
- name: Demonstrate the debug module
  hosts: ansibletest
  user: root
  vars:
    hostcount: 5
  tasks:
    - name: Print interface
      debug: msg="{{ item }}"
      with_items: ansible_interfaces
```

The preceding code gives the following output:

```
PLAY [Demonstrate the debug module] *********************************

GATHERING FACTS *****************************************************
ok: [ansibletest]

TASK: [Print IP address] ********************************************
ok: [ansibletest] => (item=lo) => {"item": "lo", "msg": "lo"}
ok: [ansibletest] => (item=eth0) => {"item": "eth0", "msg": "eth0"}

PLAY RECAP **********************************************************
ansibletest                    : ok=2    changed=0    unreachable=0
failed=0
```

As you can see the `debug` module is easy to use to see the current value of a variable during the play.

The verbose mode

Your other option for debugging is the verbose option. When running Ansible with verbose, it prints out all the values that were returned by each module after it runs. This is especially useful if you are using the `register` keyword introduced in the previous section. To run `ansible-playbook` in verbose mode, simply add `--verbose` to your command line as follows:

```
ansible-playbook --verbose playbook.yml
```

The check mode

In addition to the verbose mode, Ansible also includes a **check** mode and a **diff** mode. You can use the check mode by adding `--check` to the command line, and `--diff` to use the diff mode. The check mode instructs Ansible to walk through the play without actually making any changes to remote systems. This allows you to obtain a listing of the changes that Ansible plans to make to the configured system.

> It is important here to note that the check mode of Ansible is not perfect. Any modules that do not implement the check feature are skipped. Additionally, if a module is skipped that provides more variables, or the variables depend on a module actually changing something (like file size), then they will not be available. This is an obvious limitation when using the command or shell modules.

The diff mode shows the changes that are made by the `template` module. This limitation is because the template file only works with text files. If you were to provide a diff of a binary file from the copy module, the result would almost be unreadable. The diff mode also works with the check mode to show you the planned changes that were not made due to being in check mode.

The pause module

Another technique is to use the `pause` module to pause the playbook while you examine the configured machine as it runs. This way you can see changes that the modules have made at the current position in the play, and then watch while it continues with the rest of the play.

Summary

In this chapter we explored the more advanced details of writing playbooks. You should now be able to use features such as delegation, looping, conditionals, and fact registration to make your plays much easier to maintain and edit. We also looked at how to access information from other hosts, configure the environment for a module, and gather data from external sources. Finally we covered some techniques for debugging plays that are not behaving as expected.

In the next chapter we will be covering how to use Ansible in a larger environment. It will include methods for improving the performance of your playbooks that may be taking a long time to execute. We will also cover a few more features that make plays maintainable, particularly splitting them into many parts by purpose.

4
Larger Projects

Until now, we have been looking at single plays in one playbook file. This approach will work for simple infrastructures, or when using Ansible as a simple deployment mechanism. However, if you have a large and complicated infrastructure, then you will need to take actions to prevent things from going out of control. This chapter will include the following topics:

- Separating your playbooks into different files, and including them from some other location
- Using roles to include multiple files that perform a similar function
- Methods for increasing the speed at which Ansible configures your machines

Includes

One of the first issues you will face with a complex infrastructure is that your playbooks will rapidly increase in size. Large playbooks can become difficult to read and maintain. Ansible allows you to combat this problem by the way of includes.

Includes allow you to split your plays into multiple sections. You can then include each section from other plays. This allows you to have several different parts built for a different purpose, all included in a main play.

There are four types of includes, namely variable includes, playbook includes, task includes, and handler includes. Including variables from an external vars_file files has been discussed already in *Chapter 2, Simple Playbooks*. The following is a summary of what each includes does:

- **Variable includes**: They allow you to put your variables in external YAML files
- **Playbook includes**: They are used to include plays from other files in a s ingle play

- **Task includes**: They let you put common tasks in other files and include them wherever required
- **Handler includes**: They let you put all your handlers in the one place

Task includes

Task includes can be used when you have a lot of common tasks that will be repeated. For example, you may have a set of tasks that removes a machine, from monitoring, and a load balancer before you can configure it. You can put these tasks in a separate YAML file, and then include them from your main task.

Task includes inherit the facts from the play they are included from. You can also provide your own variables, which are passed into the task and available for use.

Finally, task includes can have conditionals applied to them. If you do this, conditionals will separately be added to each included task. The tasks are all still included. In most cases, this is not an important distinction, but in circumstances where variables may change, it is.

The file to include as a task includes contains a list of tasks. If you assume the existence of any variables and hosts or groups, then you should state them in comments at the top. This makes reusing the file much easier.

So, if you wanted to create a bunch of users and set up their environment with their public keys, you would split out the tasks that do a single user to one file. This file would look similar to the following code:

```
---
# Requires a user variable to specify user to setup       #1
- name: Create user account        #2
  user: name={{ user }} state=present       #3

- name: Make user SSH config dir       #4
  file: path=/home/{{ user }}/.ssh owner={{ user }} group={{ user
  }} mode=0600 state=directory       #5

- name: Copy in public key       #6
  copy: src=keys/{{ user }}.pub dest=/home/{{ user
  }}/.ssh/authorized_keys mode=0600 owner={{ user }} group={{ user
    }}       #7
```

We expect that a variable named `user` will be passed to us, and that their public key will be in the `keys` directory. The account is created, the `ssh config` directory is made, and finally we can copy this in their public key. The easiest way to use this `config` file would be to include it with the `with_items` keyword we learned about in *Chapter 3, Advanced Playbooks*. This would look similar to the following code:

```
---
- hosts: ansibletest
  user: root
  tasks:
    - include: usersetup.yml user={{ item }}
      with_items:
        - mal
        - dan
        - kate
```

Handler includes

When writing Ansible playbooks, you will constantly find yourself reusing the same handlers multiple times. For instance, a handler used to restart MySQL is going to look the same everywhere. To make this easier, Ansible allows you to include other files in the handlers section. Handler includes look the same as task includes. You should make sure to include a name on each of your handlers; otherwise you will not be able to refer to them easily in your tasks. A handler include file looks similar to the following code:

```
---
- name: config sendmail
  command: make -C /etc/mail
  notify: reload sendmail

- name: config aliases
  command: newaliases
  notify: reload sendmail

- name: reload sendmail
  service: name=sendmail state=reloaded

- name: restart sendmail
  service: name=sendmail state=restarted
```

This file provides several common tasks that you would want to handle after configuring `sendmail`. By including the following handlers in their own files, you can easily reuse them whenever you need to change the `sendmail` configuration:

- The first handler regenerates the `sendmail` database's `config` file and triggers a `reload` file of `sendmail` later
- The second handler initializes the `aliases` database, and also schedules a `reload` file of `sendmail`

- The third handler reloads `sendmail`; it may be triggered by the previous two jobs, or it may be triggered directly from a task
- The fourth handler restarts `sendmail` when triggered; this is useful if you upgrade `sendmail` to a new version

> Handlers can trigger other handlers provided that they only trigger the ones specified later, instead of the triggered ones. This means, you can set up a series of cascading handlers that call each other. This saves you from having long lists of handlers in the notify section of tasks.

Using the preceding handler file is easy now. We simply need to remember that if we change a `sendmail` configuration file, then we should trigger `config sendmail`, and if we change the `aliases` file, we should trigger `config aliases`. The following code shows us an example of this:

```
---
  hosts: mailers        #1
  tasks:        #2
    - name: update sendmail        #3
      yum: name=sendmail state=latest        #4
      notify: restart sendmail        #5

    - name: configure sendmail        #6
      template: src=templates/sendmail.mc.j2
        dest=/etc/mail/sendmail.mc        #7
      notify: config sendmail        #8

  handlers:        #9
    - include: sendmailhandlers.yml        #10
```

This playbook makes sure `sendmail` is installed. If it isn't installed or if it isn't running the latest version, then it installs it. After it is updated, it schedules a restart so that we can be confident that the latest version will be running once the playbook is done. In the next step, we replace the `sendmail` configuration file with our template. If the `config` file was changed by the template then the `sendmail` configuration files will be regenerated, and finally `sendmail` will be reloaded.

Playbook includes

Playbook includes should be used when you want to include a whole set of tasks designated for a set of machines. For example, you may have a play that gathers the host keys of several machines and builds a `known_hosts` file to copy to all the machines.

While task includes allows you to include tasks, playbook includes allows you to include whole plays. This allows you to select the hosts you wish to run on, and provide handlers for notify events. Because you are including whole playbook files, you can also include multiple plays.

Playbook includes allows you to embed fully self-contained files. It is for this reason that you should provide any variables that it requires. If they depend on any particular set of hosts or groups, this should be noted in a comment at the top of the file.

This is handy when you wish to run multiple different actions at once. For example, let's say we have a playbook that switches to our DR site, named `drfailover.yml`, another named `upgradeapp.yml` that upgrades the app, another named `drfailback.yml` that fails back, and finally `drupgrade.yml`. All these playbooks might be valid to use separately, but when performing a site upgrade, you will probably want to perform them all at once. You can do this as shown in the following code:

```
---
- include "drfailover.yml"       #1
- include "upgradeapp.yml"       #2
- include "drfailback.yml"       #3

- name: Notify management       #4
  hosts: local       #5
  tasks:       #6
    - local_action: mail to="mgmt-team@example.com" msg='The
      application has been upgraded and is now live'       #7

- include "drupgrade.yml"       #8
```

As you can see, you can put full plays in the playbooks that you are including other playbooks into.

Roles

If your playbooks start expanding beyond what includes can help you solve, or you start gathering a large number of templates, you may want to use roles. Roles in Ansible allow you to group files together in a defined format. They are essentially an extension to includes that handles a few things automatically, and this helps you organize them inside your repository.

Roles allows you to place your variables, files, tasks, templates, and handlers in a folder, and then easily include them. You can also include other roles from within roles, which effectively creates a tree of dependencies. Similar to task includes, they can have variables passed to them. Using these features, you should be able to build self-contained roles that are easy to share with others.

Roles are commonly set up to be services provided by machines, but they can also be daemons, options, or simply characteristics. Things you may want to configure in a role are as follows:

- Webservers, such as Nginx or Apache
- Messages of the day customized for the security level of the machine
- Database servers running PostgreSQL or MySQL

To manage roles in Ansible perform the following steps:

1. Create a folder named `roles` with your playbooks.
2. In the `roles` folder, make a folder for each role that you would like.
3. In the folder for each role, make folders named `files`, `handlers`, `meta`, `tasks`, `templates`, and finally `vars`. If you aren't going to use all these, you can leave the ones you don't need off. Ansible will silently ignore any missing files or directories when using roles.
4. In your playbooks, add the keyword roles followed by a list of roles that you would like to apply to the hosts.
5. For example, if you had the `common`, `apache`, `website1`, and `website2` roles, your directory structure would look similar to the following example. The `site.yml` file is for reconfiguring the entire site, and the `webservers1.yml` and `webservers2.yml` files are for configuring each web server farm.

```
.
├── inventory.ini
├── roles
│   ├── apache
│   │   ├── files
│   │   ├── handlers
│   │   │   └── main.yml
│   │   ├── meta
│   │   ├── tasks
│   │   │   └── main.yml
│   │   ├── templates
│   │   │   └── httpd.conf.j2
│   │   └── vars
│   │       └── main.yml
│   ├── common
│   │   ├── files
│   │   │   └── bashrc
│   │   ├── handlers
│   │   ├── meta
│   │   ├── tasks
│   │   │   └── main.yml
│   │   ├── templates
│   │   │   └── motd.j2
│   │   └── vars
│   │       └── main.yml
│   ├── website1
│   │   ├── files
│   │   ├── handlers
│   │   │   └── main.yml
│   │   ├── meta
│   │   ├── tasks
│   │   │   └── main.yml
│   │   ├── templates
│   │   │   └── environment.yml.j2
│   │   │   └── website1.conf.j2
│   │   └── vars
│   │       └── main.yml
│   └── website2
│       ├── files
│       ├── handlers
│       │   └── main.yml
│       ├── meta
│       ├── tasks
│       │   └── main.yml
│       ├── templates
│       │   └── environment.yml.j2
│       │   └── website2.conf.j2
│       └── vars
│           └── main.yml
├── website1.yml
└── website2.yml
```

The following file is what could be in `website1.yml`. It shows a playbook that applies the `common`, `apache`, and `website1` roles to the `website1` group in the inventory. The `website1` role is included using a more verbose format that allows us to pass variables to the role:

```
---
- name: Setup servers for website1.example.com
  hosts: website1
  roles:
    - common
    - apache
    - { role: website1, port: 80 }
```

For the role named `common`, Ansible will then try to load `roles/common/tasks/main.yml` as a task include, `roles/common/handlers/main.yml` as a handler include, and `roles/common/vars/main.yml` as a variable file include. If all of these files are missing, Ansible will throw an error; however, if one of the files exists then the others, if missing, will be ignored. The following directories are used by a default install of Ansible. Other directories may be used by different modules:

Directory	**Description**
`tasks`	The `tasks` folder should contain a `main.yml` file, which should include a list of the tasks for this role. Any task includes that are contained in these roles will look for their files in this folder also. This allows you to split a large number of tasks into separate files, and use other features of task includes.
`files`	The `files` folder is the default location for files in the roles that are used by the copy or the script module.
`templates`	The `templates` directory is the location where the template module will automatically look for the jinja2 templates included in the roles.
`handlers`	The `handlers` folder should contain a `main.yml` file, which specifies the handlers for the roles, and any includes in that folder will also look for the files in the same location..
`vars`	The `vars` folder should contain a `main.yml` file, which contains the variables for this role.

Directory	Description
`meta`	The `meta` folder should contain a `main.yml` file. This file can contain settings for the role, and a list of its dependencies. This feature is available only in Ansible 1.3 and above.
`default`	You should use the `default` folder if you are expecting variables to be sent to this roles, and you want to make them optional. A `main.yml` file in this folder is read, to get the initial values for variables that can be overridden by variables, which are passed from the playbook calling the role. This feature is only available in Ansible 1.3 and above.

When using roles, the behavior of the copy, the template, and the script modules is slightly altered. Instead of searching for files by looking from the directory in which the playbook file is located, Ansible will look for the files in the location of the role. For example, if you are using a role named `common`, these modules will change to the following behavior:

- The copy module will look for files in `roles/common/files`.
- The template module will look for templates in `roles/common/templates`.
- The script module will look for files in `roles/common/files`.
- Other modules may decide to look for their data in other folders inside `roles/common/`. The documentation for modules can be retrieved using `ansible-doc`, as was discussed in the *Module help* section of *Chapter 1, Getting Started* with Ansible.

New features in 1.3

There are two features in Ansible 1.3 that were alluded to previously in the chapter. The first feature is the `metadata` roles. They allow you to specify that your role depends on other roles. For example, if the application that you are deploying needs to send mail, your role could depend on a `Postfix` role. This would mean that before the application is set up and installed, `Postfix` will be installed and set up.

The `meta/main.yml` file would look similar to the following code:

```
---
allow_duplicates: no
dependencies:
  - apache
```

The allow_duplicates line is set to no, which is the default. If you set this to no, Ansible will not run a role the second time, if it is included twice with the same arguments. If you set it to yes, it will repeat the role even if it has run before. You can leave it off instead of setting it to no.

Dependencies are specified in the same format as roles. This means, you can pass variables here; either static values or variables that are passed to the current role.

The second feature included with Ansible 1.3 is variable default values. If you place a main.yml file in the defaults directory for the role, these variables will be read into the role; however they can be overridden by variables in the vars/main.yml file, or the variables that are passed to the role when it is included. This allows you to make passing variables to the role optional. These files look exactly like other variable files. For example, if you used a variable named port in your role, and you wanted to default it to port 80, your defaults/main.yml file would look similar to the following code:

```
---
port: 80
```

Speeding things up

As you add more and more machines and services to your Ansible configuration, you will find things getting slower and slower. Fortunately, there are several tricks you can use to make Ansible work on a bigger scale.

Tags

Ansible tags are features that allow you to select which parts of a playbook you need to run, and which should be skipped. While Ansible modules are idempotent and will automatically skip if there are no changes, this often requires a connection to the remote hosts. The yum module is often quite slow in determining if a module is the latest, as it will need to refresh all the repositories.

If you know you don't need certain actions to be run, you can select only run modules that have been tagged with a particular tag. This doesn't even try to run the module, it simply skips over it. This will save time on almost all the modules even if there is nothing to be done.

Let's say you have a machine which has a large number of shell accounts, but also several services set up to run on it. Now, imagine that a single user's SSH key has been compromised and needs to be removed immediately. Instead of running the entire playbook, or rewriting the playbooks to only include the steps necessary to remove that key, you could simply run the existing playbooks with the SSH keys tag, and it would only run the steps necessary to copy out the new keys, instantly skipping anything else.

This is particularly useful if you have a playbook with playbook includes in it that covers your whole infrastructure. With this setup, you can quickly deploy security patches, change passwords, and revoke keys across your entire infrastructure as quickly as possible.

Tagging tasks is really easy; simply add a key named `tag`, and set its value to a list of the tags you want to give it. The following code shows us how to do this:

```
---
- name: Install and setup our webservers        #1
  hosts: webservers       #2
  tasks:       #3
  - name: install latest software       #4
    action: yum name=$item state=latest       #5
    notify: restart apache       #6
    tags:       #7
      - patch       #8
    with_items:       #9
    - httpd       #10
    - webalizer       #11

  - name: Create subdirectories       #12
    action: file dest=/var/www/html/$item state=directory mode=755
      owner=apache group=apache       #13
    tags:       #14
      - deploy       #15
    with_items:       #16
      - pub       #17

  - name: Copy in web files       #18
    action: copy src=website/$item dest=/var/www/html/$item
      mode=755 owner=apache group=apache       #19
    tags:       #20
      - deploy       #21
```

```
    with_items:       #22
      - index.html       #23
      - logo.png       #24
      - style.css       #25
      - app.js       #26
      - pub/index.html       #27

  - name: Copy webserver config       #28
    tags:       #29
      - deploy       #30
      - config       #31
    action: copy src=website/httpd.conf
      dest=/etc/httpd/conf/httpd.conf mode=644 owner=root
        group=root       #32
    notify: reload apache       #33

  - name: set apache to start on startup       #34
    action: service name=httpd state=started enabled=yes       #35

  handlers:       #36
  - name: reload apache       #37
    service: name=httpd state=reloaded       #38

  - name: restart apache       #39
    service: name=httpd state=restarted       #40
```

This play defines the `patch`, `deploy`, and `config` tags. If you know which operation you wish to do in advance, you can run Ansible with the correct argument, only running the operations you choose. If you don't supply a tag on the command line, the default is to run every task. For example, if you want Ansible to only run the tasks tagged as `deploy`, you would run the following command:

```
$ ansible-playbook webservers.yml --tags deploy
```

In addition to working on discrete tasks, tags are also available to roles, which makes Ansible apply only the roles for the tags that have been supplied on the command line. You apply them similarly to the way they are applied to tasks. For example, refer to the following code:

```
---
- hosts: website1
  roles:
    - common
    - { role: apache, tags: ["patch"] }
    - { role: website2, tags: ["deploy", "patch"] }
```

In the preceding code, the `common` role does not get any tags, and will not be run if there are any tags applied. If the `patch` tag is applied, the `apache` and `website2` roles will be applied, but not `common`. If the `deploy` tag is applied; only the `website2` tag will be run. This will shorten the time required to patch servers or run deployments as the unnecessary steps will be completely skipped.

Ansible's pull mode

Ansible includes a pull mode which can drastically improve the scalability of your playbooks. So far we have only covered using Ansible to configure another machine over SSH. This is a contrast to Ansible's pull mode, which runs on the host that you wish to configure. Since `ansible-pull` runs on the machine that it is configuring, it doesn't need to make connections to other machines and runs much faster. In this mode, you provide your configuration in a `git` repository which Ansible downloads and uses to configure your machine.

You should use Ansible's pull mode in the following situations:

- Your node might not be available when configuring them, such as members of auto-scaling server farms
- You have a large amount of machines to configure and even with large values of `forks`, it would take a long time to configure them all
- You want machines to update their configuration automatically when the repository changes
- You want to run Ansible on a machine that may not have network access yet, such as in a kick start post install

However, pull mode does have the following disadvantages that make it unsuitable for certain circumstances:

- To connect to other machines and gather variables, or copy a file you need to have credentials on the managed nodes
- You need to co-ordinate the running of the playbook across a server farm; for example, if you could only take three servers offline at a time
- The servers are behind strict firewalls that don't allow incoming SSH connections from the nodes you use to configure them for Ansible

Pull mode doesn't require anything special in your playbooks, but it does require some setup on the nodes you want configured. In some circumstances, you could do this using Ansible's normal push mode. Here is a small play to setup play mode on a machine:

```
---
- name: Ansible Pull Mode       #1
  hosts: pullhosts      #2
  tasks:       #3
    - name: Setup EPEL       #4
      action: command rpm -ivh
        http://download.fedoraproject.org/pub/epel/6/i386/epel-
          release-6-8.noarch.rpm
            creates=/etc/yum.repos.d/epel.repo       #5

    - name: Install Ansible + Dependencies       #6
      yum: name={{ item }} state=latest enablerepo=epel       #7
      with_items:       #8
      - ansible       #9
      - git-core       #10

    - name: Make directory to put downloaded playbooks in       #11
      file: state=directory path=/opt/ansiblepull       #12

    - name: Setup cron       #13
      cron: name="ansible-pull" user=root minute="*/5"
        state=present job="ansible-pull -U
          https://git.int.example.com.com/gitrepos/ansiblepull.git
            -D /opt/ansiblepull {{ inventory_hostname_short
              }}.yml"       #14
```

In this example, we performed the following steps:

- First, we( )installed and set up **EPEL**. This is a repository with extra software for CentOS. Ansible is available in the EPEL repository.
- Next, we installed Ansible, making sure to enable the EPEL repository.
- Then, we created a directory for Ansible's pull mode to put the playbooks in. Keeping these files around means you don't need to download the whole `git` repository the whole time; only updates are required.
- Finally, we set up a `cron` job that will try to run the `ansible-pull` mode config every five minutes.

The preceding code downloads the repository off an internal HTTPS `git` server. If you want to download the repository instead of SSH, you will need to add a step to install SSH keys, or generate keys and copy them to the `git` machine.

Summary

In this chapter, we have covered the techniques required when moving from a simple setup to a larger deployment. We discussed how to separate your playbook into multiple parts using includes. We then looked at how we can package up related includes and automatically include them all at once using roles. Finally we discussed pull mode, which allows you to automate the deployment of playbooks on the remote node itself.

In the next chapter, we will cover writing your own modules. We start this by building a simple module using bash scripting. We then look at how Ansible searches for modules, and how to make it find your own custom ones. Then, we take a look at how you can use Python to write more advanced modules using features that Ansible provides. Finally, we will write a script that configures Ansible to pull its inventory from an external source.

5
Custom Modules

Until now we have been working solely with the tools provided to us by Ansible. This does afford us a lot of power, and make many things possible. However, if you have something particularly complex or if you find yourself using the script module a lot, you will probably want to learn how to extend Ansible.

In this chapter you will learn the following topics:

- How to write modules in Bash scripting or Python
- Using custom modules that you have developed
- Writing a script to use an external data source as an inventory

Often when you approach something complex in Ansible, you write a script module. The issue with script modules is that you can't process their output, or trigger handlers based on their output easily. So, although the script module works in some cases, using a module can be better.

Use a module instead of writing a script when:

- You don't want to run the script every single time
- You need to process the output
- Your script needs to make facts
- You need to send complex variables as arguments

If you want to start writing modules, you should check ( )out the Ansible repository. If you want your module to work with a particular version, you should also switch to that version to ensure compatibility. The following commands will set you up to develop modules for Ansible 1.3.0. Checking out the Ansible code gives you access to a handy script that we will use later to test our modules. We will also make this script executable in anticipation of its use later in the chapter.

```
$ git clone (https://github.com/ansible/ansible.git)
$ cd ansible
$ git checkout v1.3.0
$ chmod +x hacking/test-module
```

Writing a module in Bash

Ansible allows you to write modules in any language that you prefer. Although most modules in Ansible work with JSON, you are allowed to use shortcuts if you don't have any JSON parsing facilities available. Ansible will hand you arguments in their original key value forms, if they were provided in that format. If complex arguments are provided, you will receive JSON-encoded data. You could parse this using something like jsawk (`https://github.com/micha/jsawk`) or jq (`http://stedolan.github.io/jq/`), but only if they are installed on your remote machine.

Ansible doesn't yet have a module that lets you change the hostname of a system with the `hostname` command. So let's write one. We will start just printing the current hostname and then expand the script from there. Here is what that simple module looks like:

```
#!/bin/bash

HOSTNAME="$(hostname)"

echo "hostname=${HOSTNAME}"
```

If you have written Bash scripts before, this should seem extremely basic. Essentially what we are doing is grabbing the hostname and printing it out in a key value form. Now that we have written the first cut of the module, we should test it out.

To test the Ansible modules, we use the script that we ran the `chmod` command on earlier. This command simply runs your module, records the output, and returns it to you. It also shows how Ansible interpreted the output of the module. The command that we will use looks like the following:

```
ansible/hacking/test-module -m ./hostname
```

The output of the previous command should look like this:

```
* module boilerplate substitution not requested in module, line
numbers will be unaltered
***********************************
RAW OUTPUT
hostname=admin01.int.example.com


***********************************
PARSED OUTPUT
{
    "hostname": "admin01.int.example.com"
}
```

Ignore the notice at the top, it does not apply to modules built with bash. You can see the raw output that our script sent, which looks exactly the way we expected. The test script also gives you the parsed output. In our example, we are using the short output format and we can see here that Ansible is correctly interpreting it into the JSON that it normally accepts from modules.

Let's expand out the module to allow setting the `hostname`. We should write it so that it doesn't make any changes unless it is required, and lets Ansible know whether changes were made or not. This is actually pretty simple for the small command that we are writing. The new script should look something like this:

```
#!/bin/bash

set -e

# This is potentially dangerous
source ${1}

OLDHOSTNAME="$(hostname)"
CHANGED="False"

if [ ! -z "$hostname" -a "${hostname}x" != "${OLDHOSTNAME}x" ];
  then
  hostname $hostname
  OLDHOSTNAME="$hostname"
  CHANGED="True"
fi

echo "hostname=${OLDHOSTNAME} changed=${CHANGED}"
exit 0
```

The previous script works like this:

1. We set Bash's exit on error mode, so that we don't have to deal with errors from hostname. Bash will automatically exit on failure with its exit code. This will signal Ansible that something went wrong.
2. We source the argument file. This file is passed from Ansible as the first argument to the script. It contains the arguments that were sent to our module. Because we are sourcing the file, this could be used to run arbitrary commands; however, Ansible can already do this, so it's not that much of a security issue.
3. We collect the old hostname and default `CHANGED` to `False`. This allows us to see if our module needs to perform any changes.
4. We check if we were sent a new hostname to set, and check if that hostname is different from the one that is currently set.
5. If both those tests are true, we try to change the hostname, and set `CHANGED` to `True`.
6. Finally, we output the results and exit. This includes the current hostname and whether we made changes or not.

Changing the hostname on a Unix machine requires root privileges. So while testing this script, you need to make sure to run it as the root user. Let's test this script using `sudo` to see if it works. This is the command you will use:

```
sudo ansible/hacking/test-module -m ./hostname -a
  'hostname=test.example.com'
```

If `test.example.com` is not the current hostname of the machine, you should get the following as the output:

```
* module boilerplate substitution not requested in module, line
numbers will be unaltered
***********************************
RAW OUTPUT
hostname=test.example.com changed=True


***********************************
PARSED OUTPUT
{
    "changed": true,
    "hostname": "test.example.com"
}
```

As you can see, our output is being parsed correctly, and the module claims that changes have been made to the system. You can check this yourself with the hostname command. Now, run the module for the second time with the same hostname. You should see an output that looks like this:

```
* module boilerplate substitution not requested in module, line
numbers will be unaltered
***********************************
RAW OUTPUT
hostname=test.example.com changed=False


***********************************
PARSED OUTPUT
{
    "changed": false,
    "hostname": "test.example.com"
}
```

Again, we see that the output was parsed correctly. This time, however, the module claims to not have made any changes, which is what we expect. You can also check this with the `hostname` command.

Using a module

Now that we have written our very first module for Ansible, we should give it a go in a playbook. Ansible looks at several places for its modules: first it looks at the place specified in the `library` key in its `config` file (`/etc/ansible/ansible.cfg`), next it will look in the location specified using the `--module-path` argument in the command line, then it will look in the same directory as the playbook for a `library` directory containing modules, and finally it will look in the library directories for any roles that may be set.

Let's create a playbook that uses our new module and place it in a library directory in the same place so that we can see it in action. Here is a playbook that uses the `hostname` module:

```
---
- name: Test the hostname file
  hosts: testmachine
  tasks:
    - name: Set the hostname
      hostname: hostname=testmachine.example.com
```

Then create a directory named `library` in the same directory as the playbook file. Place the `hostname` module inside the library. Your directory layout should look like this:

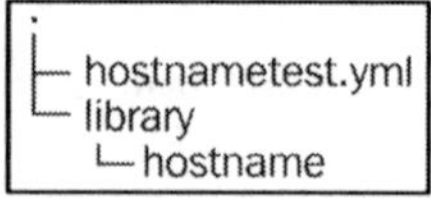

Now when you run the playbook, it will find the `hostname` module in the `library` directory and execute it. You should see an output like this:

```
PLAY [Test the hostname file] ****************************************

GATHERING FACTS ******************************************************
ok: [ansibletest]

TASK: [Set the hostname] *********************************************
changed: [ansibletest]

PLAY RECAP ***********************************************************
ansibletest                    : ok=2    changed=1    unreachable=0
failed=0
```

Running it again should change the result from `changed` to `ok`. Congratulations, you have now created and executed your very first module. This module is very simple right now, but you could extend it to know about the `hostname` file, or other methods to configure the hostname at boot time.

Writing modules in Python

All of the modules that are distributed with Ansible are written in Python. Because Ansible is also written in Python, these modules can directly integrate with Ansible. This increases the speed at which they can run. Here are a few other reasons why you might write modules in Python:

- Modules written in Python can use boilerplate, which reduces the amount of code required
- Python modules can provide documentation to be used by Ansible
- Arguments to your module are handled automatically

- Output is automatically converted to JSON for you
- Ansible upstream only accepts plugins using Python with the boilerplate code included

You can still build Python modules without this integration by parsing the arguments and outputting JSON yourself. However, with all the things you get for free, it would be hard to make a case for it.

Let's build a Python module that lets us change the currently running init level of the system. There is a Python module called `pyutmp` that will let us parse the `utmp` file. Unfortunately, since Ansible modules have to be contained in a single file, we can't use it unless we know it will be installed on the remote systems, so we will resort to using the `runlevel` command and parsing its output. Setting the runlevel can be done with the `init` command.

The first step is to figure out what arguments and features the module supports. For the sake of simplicity, let's have our module only accept one argument. We'll use the argument `runlevel` to get the runlevel the user wants to change to. To do this, we instantiate the `AnsibleModule` class with our data.

```
module = AnsibleModule(
  argument_spec = dict(
    runlevel=dict(default=None, type='str')
  )
)
```

Now we need to implement the actual guts of the module. The module object that we created previously provides us with a few shortcuts. There are three that we will be using in the next step. As there are way too many methods to document here, you can see the whole `AnsibleModule` class and all the available helper functions in `lib/ansible/module_common.py`.

- `run_command`: This method is used to launch external commands and retrieve the return code, the output from `stdout`, and also the output from `stderr`.
- `exit_json`: This method is used to return data to Ansible when the module has completed successfully.
- `fail_json`: This method is used to signal a failure to Ansible, with an error message and return code.

The following code actually manages the init level of the system. Comments have been included in the following code to explain what it does.

```
def main():      #1
  module = AnsibleModule(     #2
    argument_spec = dict(     #3
```

```
        runlevel=dict(default=None, type='str')     #4
      )     #5
    )     #6

    # Ansible helps us run commands     #7
    rc, out, err = module.run_command('/sbin/runlevel')     #8
    if rc != 0:     #9
      module.fail_json(msg="Could not determine current runlevel.",
        rc=rc, err=err)     #10

    # Get the runlevel, exit if its not what we expect     #11
    last_runlevel, cur_runlevel = out.split(' ', 1)     #12
    cur_runlevel = cur_runlevel.rstrip()     #13
    if len(cur_runlevel) > 1:     #14
      module.fail_json(msg="Got unexpected output from runlevel.",
        rc=rc)     #15

    # Do we need to change anything     #16
    if module.params['runlevel'] is None or
      module.params['runlevel'] == cur_runlevel:     #17
      module.exit_json(changed=False, runlevel=cur_runlevel)     #18

    # Check if we are root     #19
    uid = os.geteuid()     #20
    if uid != 0:     #21
      module.fail_json(msg="You need to be root to change the
        runlevel")     #22

    # Attempt to change the runlevel     #23
    rc, out, err = module.run_command('/sbin/init %s' %
      module.params['runlevel'])     #24
    if rc != 0:     #25
      module.fail_json(msg="Could not change runlevel.", rc=rc,
        err=err)     #26

    # Tell ansible the results     #27
    module.exit_json(changed=True, runlevel=cur_runlevel)     #28
```

There is one final thing to add to the boilerplate to let Ansible know that it needs to dynamically add the integration code into our module. This is the magic that lets us use the `AnsibleModule` class and enables our tight integration with Ansible. The boilerplate code needs to be placed right at the bottom of the file, with no code afterwards. The code to do this looks as follows:

```
# include magic from lib/ansible/module_common.py
#<<INCLUDE_ANSIBLE_MODULE_COMMON>>
main()
```

So, finally, we have the code for our module built. Putting it all together, it should look like the following code:

```
#!/usr/bin/python     #1
# -*- coding: utf-8 -*-     #2

import os     #3

def main():     #4
  module = AnsibleModule(     #5
    argument_spec = dict(     #6
      runlevel=dict(default=None, type='str'),     #7
    ),     #8
  )     #9

  # Ansible helps us run commands     #10
  rc, out, err = module.run_command('/sbin/runlevel')     #11
  if rc != 0:     #12
    module.fail_json(msg="Could not determine current runlevel.",
      rc=rc, err=err)     #13

  # Get the runlevel, exit if its not what we expect     #14
  last_runlevel, cur_runlevel = out.split(' ', 1)     #15
  cur_runlevel = cur_runlevel.rstrip()     #16
  if len(cur_runlevel) > 1:     #17
    module.fail_json(msg="Got unexpected output from runlevel.",
      rc=rc)     #18

  # Do we need to change anything     #19
  if (module.params['runlevel'] is None or
    module.params['runlevel'] == cur_runlevel):     #20
    module.exit_json(changed=False, runlevel=cur_runlevel)     #21

  # Check if we are root     #22
  uid = os.geteuid()     #23
  if uid != 0:     #24
    module.fail_json(msg="You need to be root to change the
      runlevel")     #25

  # Attempt to change the runlevel     #26
  rc, out, err = module.run_command('/sbin/init %s' %
    module.params['runlevel'])     #27
  if rc != 0:     #28
```

```
        module.fail_json(msg="Could not change runlevel.", rc=rc,
          err=err)     #29

    # Tell ansible the results     #30
    module.exit_json(changed=True, runlevel=cur_runlevel)     #31

# include magic from lib/ansible/module_common.py     #32
#<<INCLUDE_ANSIBLE_MODULE_COMMON>>     #33
main()     #34
```

You can test this module the same way you tested the Bash module with the `test-module` script. However, you need to be careful because if you run it with `sudo`, you might reboot your machine or alter the init level to something you don't want. This module is probably better tested by using Ansible itself on a remote test machine. We follow the same process as described in the *Using a module* section earlier in this chapter. We create a playbook that uses the module, and then place the module in a library directory that has been made in the same directory as the playbook. Here is the playbook we should use:

```
---
- name: Test the new init module
  hosts: testmachine
  user: root
  tasks:
    - name: Set the init level to 5
      init: runlevel=5
```

Now you should be able to try and run this on a remote machine. The first time you run it, if the machine is not already in runlevel 5, you should see it change the runlevel. Then you should be able to run it for a second time to see that nothing has changed. You might also want to check to make sure the module fails correctly when not run as root.

External inventories

In the first chapter we saw how Ansible needs an inventory file, so that it knows where its hosts are and how to access them. Ansible also allows you to specify a script that allows you to fetch the inventory from another source. External inventory scripts can be written in any language that you like as long as they output valid JSON.

An external inventory script has to accept two different calls from Ansible. If called with `-list`, it must return a list of all the available groups and the hosts in them. Additionally, it may be called with `--host`. In this case, the second argument will be a hostname and the script is expected to return a list of variables for that host. All the outputs are expected in JSON, so you should use a language that supports it naturally.

Let's write a module that takes a CSV file listing all your machines and presents this to Ansible as an inventory. This will be handy if you have a CMDB that allows you to export your machine list as CSV, or for someone who keeps records of their machines in Excel. Additionally, it doesn't require any dependencies outside Python, as a CSV processing module is already included with Python. This really just parses the CSV file into the right data structures and prints them out as JSON data structures. The following is an example CSV file we wish to process; you may wish to customize it for the machines in your environment:

```
Group,Host,Variables
test,example,ansible_ssh_user=root
test,localhost,connection=local
```

This file needs to be converted into two different JSON outputs. When `--list` is called, we need to output the whole thing in a form that looks like this:

```
{"test": ["example", "localhost"]}
```

And when it is called with the arguments `--host example`, it should return this:

```
{"ansible_ssh_user": "root"}
```

Here is the script that opens a file named `machines.csv` and produces the dictionary of the groups if `--list` is given. Additionally, when given `--host` and a hostname, it parses that host's variables and returns them as a dictionary. The script is well-commented, so you can see what it is doing. You can run the script manually with the `--list` and `--host` arguments to confirm that it behaves correctly.

```
#!/usr/bin/env python
# -*- coding: utf-8 -*-

import sys
import csv
import json

def getlist(csvfile):
  # Init local variables
  glist = dict()
  rowcount = 0
```

```
    # Iterate over all the rows
    for row in csvfile:
      # Throw away the header (Row 0)
      if rowcount != 0:
        # Get the values out of the row
        (group, host, variables) = row

        # If this is the first time we've
        # read this group create an empty
        # list for it
        if group not in glist:
          glist[group] = list()

        # Add the host to the list
        glist[group].append(host)

      # Count the rows we've processed
      rowcount += 1

    return glist

  def gethost(csvfile, host):
    # Init local variables
    rowcount = 0

    # Iterate over all the rows
    for row in csvfile:
      # Throw away the header (Row 0)
      if rowcount != 0 and row[1] == host:
        # Get the values out of the row
        variables = dict()
        for kvpair in row[2].split():
          key, value = kvpair.split('=', 1)
          variables[key] = value

        return variables

      # Count the rows we've processed
      rowcount += 1

  command = sys.argv[1]
```

```
#Open the CSV and start parsing it
with open('machines.csv', 'r') as infile:
  result = dict()
  csvfile = csv.reader(infile)

  if command == '--list':
    result = getlist(csvfile)
  elif command == '--host':
    result = gethost(csvfile, sys.argv[2])

  print json.dumps(result)
```

You can now use this inventory script to provide the inventory when using Ansible. A quick way to test that everything is working correctly is to use the `ping` module to test the connection to all the machines. This command will not test whether the hosts are in the right groups; if you want to do that, you can use the same `ping` module command but instead of running it across all, you can simply use the group you would like to test.

```
$ ansible -i csvinventory -m ping all
```

Similar to when you used the `ping` module in *Chapter 1, Getting Started with Ansible*, you should see an output that looks like the following:

```
localhost | success >> {
  "changed": false,
  "ping": "pong"
}

example | success >> {
  "changed": false,
  "ping": "pong"
}
```

This indicates that you can connect and use Ansible on all the hosts from your inventory. You can use the same `-i` argument with `ansible-playbook` to run your playbooks with the same inventory.

Summary

Having read this chapter you should now be able to build modules using either Bash or any other languages that you know. You should be able to install modules that you have either obtained from the Internet, or written yourself. We also covered how to write modules more efficiently using the boilerplate code in Python. Finally, we wrote an inventory script that allows you to pull your inventory from an external source.

Index

E

F

G

H

I

J

L

M

O

P

R

S

T

V

W

Y

Thank you for buying

Ansible Configuration Management

About Packt Publishing

Packt, pronounced 'packed', published its first book "*Mastering phpMyAdmin for Effective MySQL Management*" in April 2004 and subsequently continued to specialize in publishing highly focused books on specific technologies and solutions.

Our books and publications share the experiences of your fellow IT professionals in adapting and customizing today's systems, applications, and frameworks. Our solution based books give you the knowledge and power to customize the software and technologies you're using to get the job done. Packt books are more specific and less general than the IT books you have seen in the past. Our unique business model allows us to bring you more focused information, giving you more of what you need to know, and less of what you don't.

Packt is a modern, yet unique publishing company, which focuses on producing quality, cutting-edge books for communities of developers, administrators, and newbies alike. For more information, please visit our website: `www.packtpub.com`.

About Packt Open Source

In 2010, Packt launched two new brands, Packt Open Source and Packt Enterprise, in order to continue its focus on specialization. This book is part of the Packt Open Source brand, home to books published on software built around Open Source licences, and offering information to anybody from advanced developers to budding web designers. The Open Source brand also runs Packt's Open Source Royalty Scheme, by which Packt gives a royalty to each Open Source project about whose software a book is sold.

Writing for Packt

We welcome all inquiries from people who are interested in authoring. Book proposals should be sent to author@packtpub.com. If your book idea is still at an early stage and you would like to discuss it first before writing a formal book proposal, contact us; one of our commissioning editors will get in touch with you.

We're not just looking for published authors; if you have strong technical skills but no writing experience, our experienced editors can help you develop a writing career, or simply get some additional reward for your expertise.

[PACKT] open source
community experience distilled
PUBLISHING

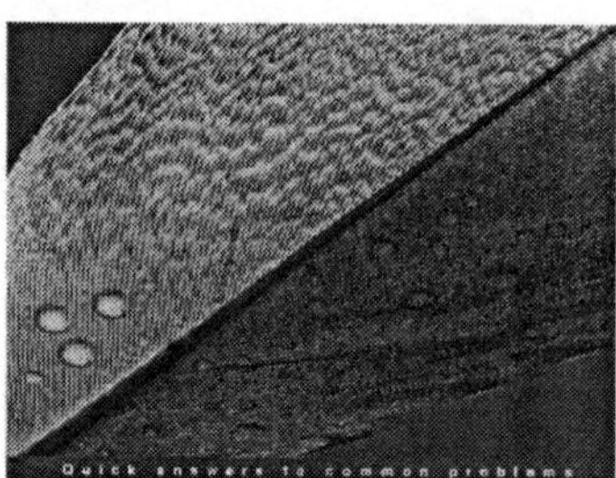

Microsoft System Center 2012 Configuration Manager: Administration Cookbook

Over 50 practical recipes to administer System Center 2012 Configuration Manager

Microsoft System Center 2012 Configuration Manager: Administration Cookbook

ISBN: 978-1-84968-494-1 Paperback: 224 pages

Over 50 practical recipes to administer System Center 2012 Configuration Manager

1. Administer System Center 2012 Configuration Manager
2. Provides fast answers to questions commonly asked by new administrators
3. Skip the why's and go straight to the how-to's
4. Gain administration tips from System Center 2012 Configuration Manager MVPs with years of experience in large corporations

---

Visual SourceSafe 2005 Software Configuration Management in Practice

ISBN: 978-1-90481-169-5 Paperback: 404 pages

Best practice management and development of Visual Studio.NET 2005 applications with this easy-to-use SCM tool from Microsoft

1. SCM fundamentals and strategies clearly explained
2. Real-world SOA example: a hotel reservation system
3. SourceSafe best practices across the complete lifecycle
4. Multiple versions, service packs and product updates.

Please check **www.PacktPub.com** for information on our titles

JBoss AS 7 Configuration, Deployment and Administration

ISBN: 978-1-84951-678-5 Paperback: 380 pages

Build a fully-functional, efficient application server using JBoss AS

1. Covers all JBoss AS 7 administration topics in a concise, practical, and understandable manner, along with detailed explanations and lots of screenshots
2. Uncover the advanced features of JBoss AS, including High Availability and clustering, integration with other frameworks, and creating complex AS domain configurations
3. Discover the new features of JBoss AS 7, which has made quite a departure from previous versions

---

Puppet 3 Cookbook

ISBN: 978-1-78216-976-5 Paperback: 274 pages

Build reliable, scalable, secure, and high-performance systems to fully utilize the power of cloud computing

1. Use Puppet 3 to take control of your servers and desktops, with detailed step-by-step instructions
2. Covers all the popular tools and frameworks used with Puppet: Dashboard, Foreman, and more
3. Teaches you how to extend Puppet with custom functions, types, and providers
4. Packed with tips and inspiring ideas for using Puppet to automate server builds, deployments, and workflows

Please check **www.PacktPub.com** for information on our titles

Lightning Source UK Ltd.
Milton Keynes UK
UKOW01f1528230714

235611UK00002B/60/P